Michael T. Ricks

Drawings, Oils, & Watercolors

1950 – 1984

ISBN: 1515096785
ISBN 13: 9781515096788

Dedicated to:

Stephen A. Ricks

an amateur artist like Dad,
and to future generations of Ricks artists.

———◆———

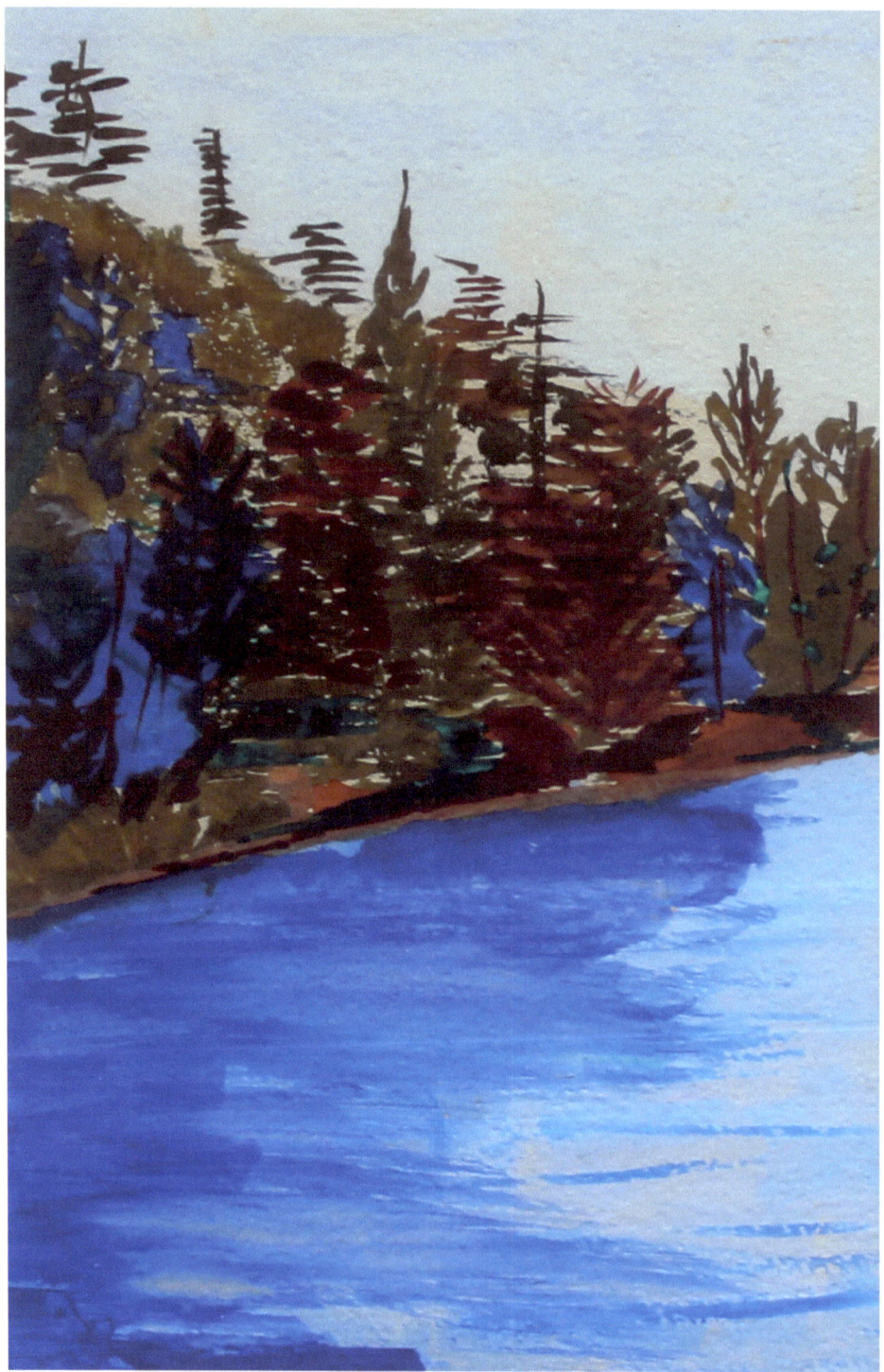

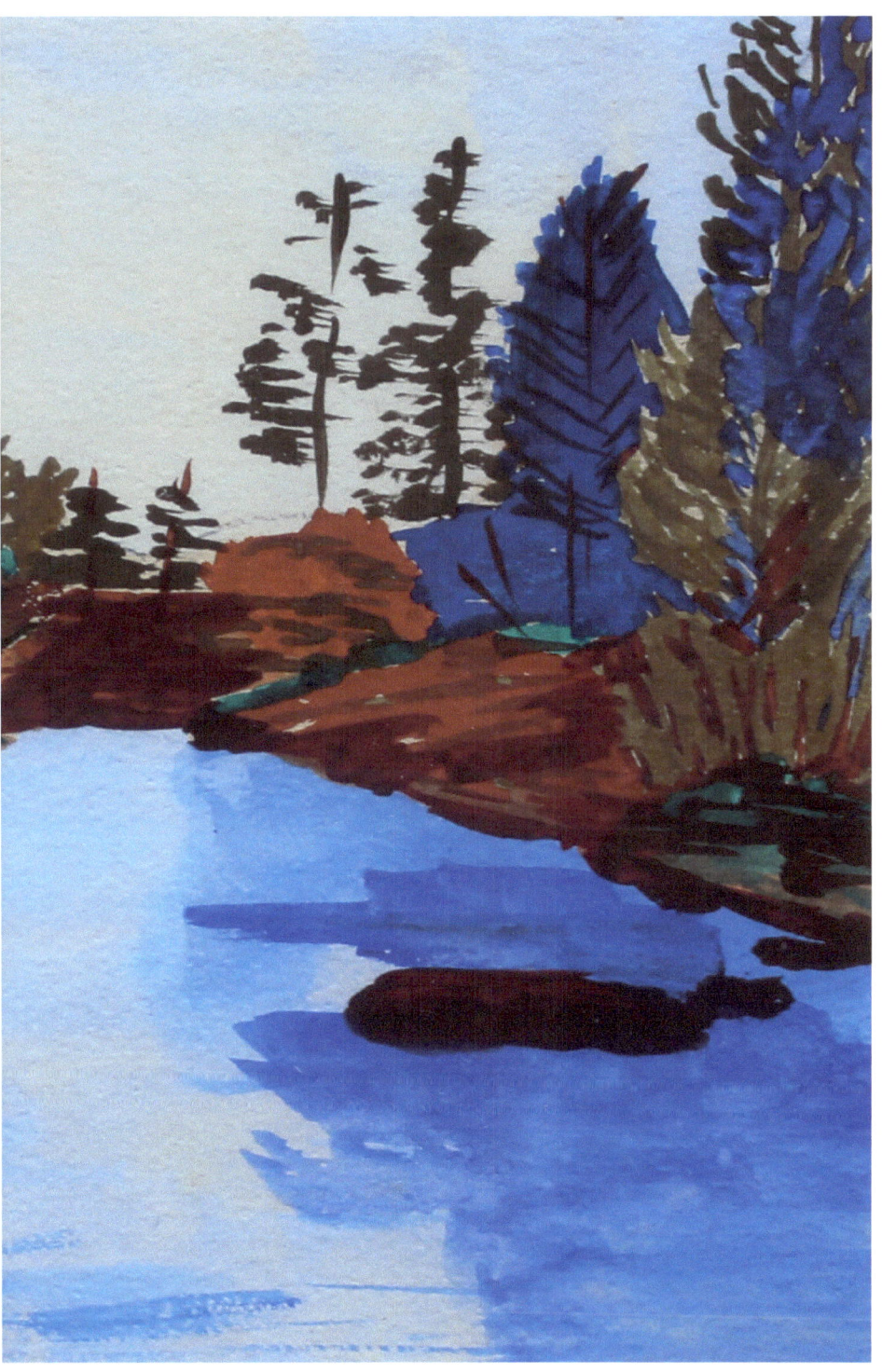

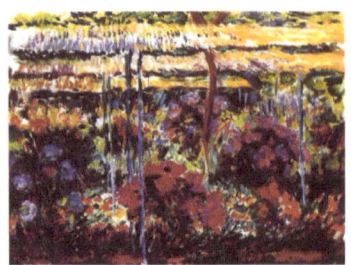

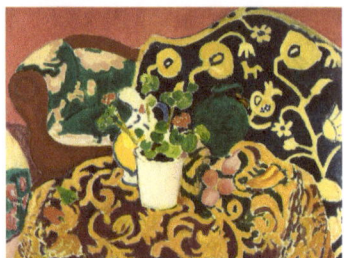

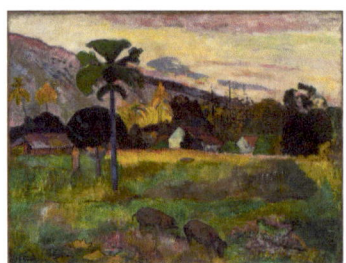

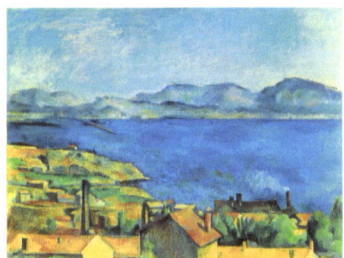

From top to bottom: Monet, Matisse,
Gauguin, Cézanne.

Mom and dad were lovers of the arts. They enjoyed reading about, traveling to, and viewing those works in museums, especially in Europe. Dad's favorite periods of art were Impressionism and Post-Impressionism. His favorite artists were Claude Monet, Paul Cezanne, Henri Matisse, and Paul Gauguin, as least these were the artists that he talked about the most.

Dad took up charcoal, oil and water color painting in the late 1950's. He began working at the 715 Miami house in the second floor den. While the room had a heating radiator in it, it was always cold in the winter. Still he pursued his hobby year around. His early work was in charcoal and four of these artworks are in the collection that the Ricks siblings have preserved.

He used a book titled "Weekend Painter" to paint from in the early years. The seascape in this catalog is one of his earliest oil paintings. Once the family began going to the Lake Michigan shore during the summer, Dad took classes at the Ox-Bow School of the Arts in Saugatuck, MI that was associated with the Art Institute of Chicago for 100 years. The Ox-Bow School of the Arts is a well-known art colony with professional artists as residents who also teach budding artists in the summer programs. Over the years, Dad spent numerous weeks in classes and painted many of the works in this catalog there. He particularly enjoyed the Saturday critiques that were conducted in the main gallery. He learned much from comments that instructors made about his and other artists work.

This was the beginning of 34 years of painting, mainly in Saugatuck, MI and in Lafayette, IN. However, he painted as well in Vero Beach, Florida when Mom and he moved there in the 1979. His work was primarily landscape with some still life subjects. He tried many media including oil and water color. Dad also used felt tipped pens and mixed media at times. His style did not attempt to develop details of a scene. He preferred to use lots of color to give an impressionistic view of his subjects. More than once he said he wanted to avoid doing "calendar art". One of the techniques learned at Ox-Bow was to squint at a scene that he was painting. This allowed him to see the overall value and composition of the subject and not to focus on the details.

Dad displayed his work at the Greater Lafayette Art Museum in Lafayette, IN and at the Central Illinois Art Exhibits in Decatur, Illinois. He received an honorable mention for a work in this collection titled Ancient Pine Root, most likely in 1965 in Lafayette, IN.

His failing eyesight prevented him from doing all that he could. Still, he left us all a fine legacy of his favorite pasttime and 45 pieces of art that we all love with many framed and hanging in our homes.

Thanks to Michael, Thomas, Theodore, Suzi, Stephen, and Alan Ricks – all children of Michael T. Ricks – for their help in preparing this catalog, as well as, thanks to Stephen for this fine Preface and Suzi for her edits.

Special thanks to James Michael Ricks, grandson and professional artist in Dublin, Ireland, who originally thought of this catalog of his grandfather's artwork. He wrote the Introduction and formatted this slim volume for publication.

Ted Ricks
Lake Oswego, OR
2015

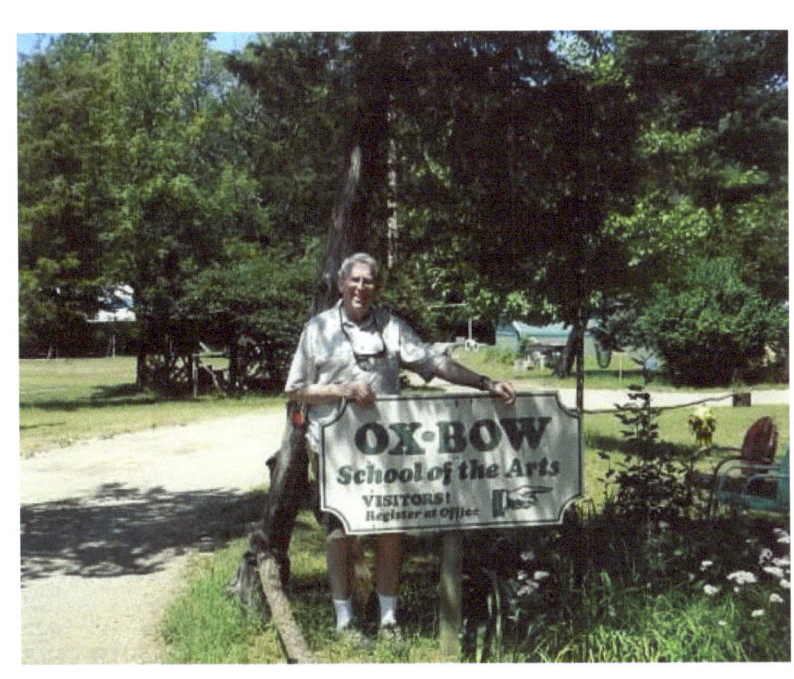

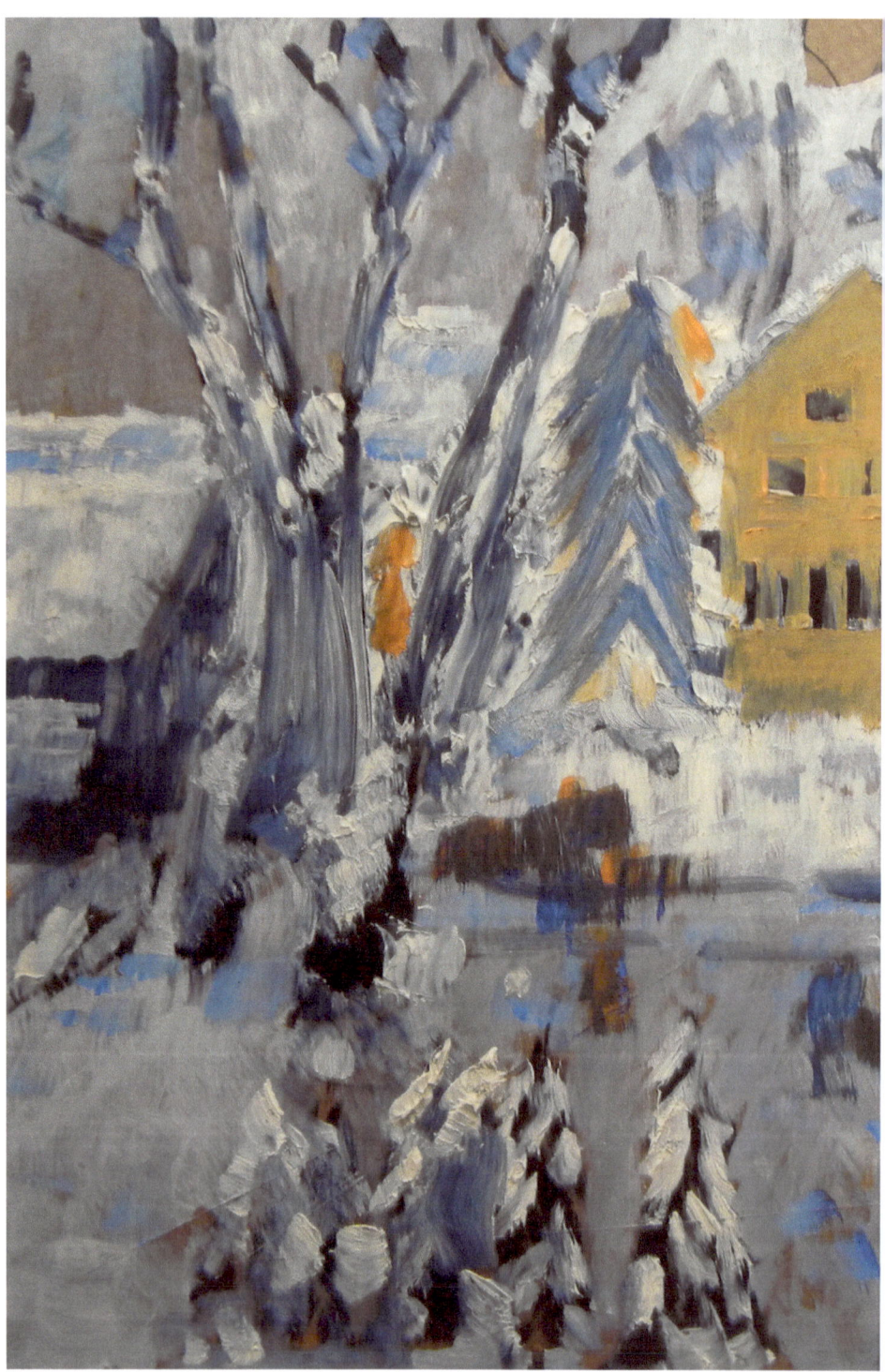

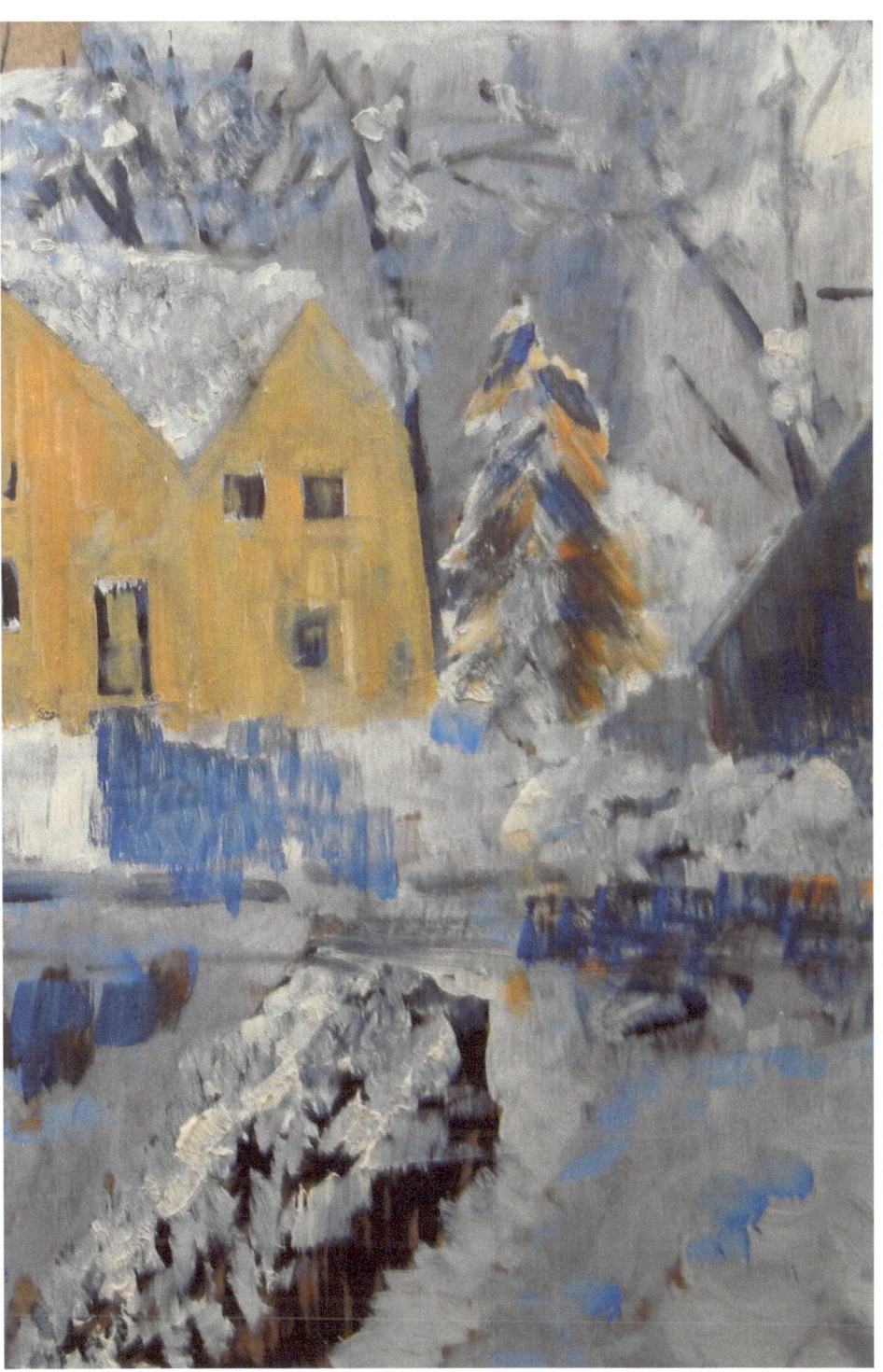

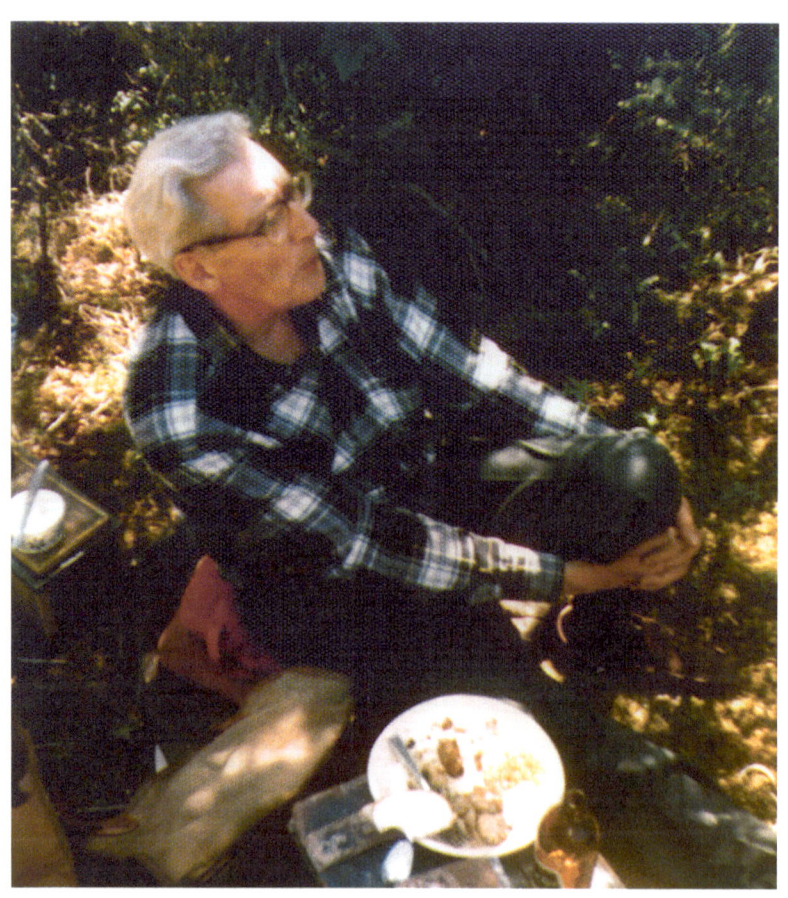

Six years ago, in the Summer of 2008, at my request, my father sent around an email titled "An inventory of Dad's paintings and watercolors." It was a call sent to his siblings to document grandfather's paintings. It was well known he was a hobbyist painter, and that his paintings had been given to his children over time. But it was not clear exactly what was there; what comprised his body of work.

Of course, there are many creatives in the extended Ricks family. From what I recall music was the default for my Dad, Aunt, and Uncles. But, as far as I know, I am the only visual artist. And being the only other artist within the family, it was of a personal interest to me. Out of a genuine/earnest curiosity, I simply hoped to see my Dad's Dad's full body of artistic work, and to create some unified understanding of his talent, the man himself, and of my lineage/heritage.

As it turns out Grandfather had a very particular taste and style. There are three distinct strands within his entirely landscape oeuvre: flora in a singular way, natural landscapes (the plural way), and architectural within the natural landscape. Using a loose gestural technique inspired by Impressionism, seen in his notable use of colour. In his best moments he demonstrates highly proficient and complex colour schemes. Strong linear forms build up and play off of loose nebulous fields of near formless colour.

His work in combination yields new understanding. Subtexts of a lawyers mind, the undercurrents and emotional impressions of a quiet, private, and sometimes intimidating man come to light. So the real joy of this 'project' has been seeing the breadth of Grandfather's work. And that his paintings are, in a way, a family treasure, bringing us together.

The process of developing this monograph has been equally connecting and important. It has been interesting in explaining to my Dad, who then conveys it to his siblings, what is needed for a simple catalogue. The assumed language (jargon, unaffectionately referred to as "International Artspeak") of my everyday life needed to be translated and broken down. Discussions of lens based ethics in a post-photographic world or the curatorial challenges of recontextualising display mechanisms were of course wholly out of place. Instead the basics needed to be covered: How to photograph art, how to categorise it, what is the object's history, was there any other documentation?

The fact of being the only two visual artists in the family could produce only a forced connection. Especially as I am more of the full-time conceptual breed, Grandfather was an amateur hobbyist (always keeping in mind that amateur is derived from the Latin *amator*, a lover of things). Yet its important to remember the real significance of art: the gratification it can bring to artist and audience alike.

Indeed, it has been a source of my inspiration as I recall Grandfather Ricks in his old age, painting for the first time in a long time in Vero Beach, Florida. It brought joy to him, but also to me and those around him. It was a sign of good health and spirit. As much as I remember him set up en plein air in the backyard with easel and paints, I also remember my father's relief as it meant Grandfather was happy and productive; his spirit is alive.

There were several works by Michael T. Ricks in our home as I grew up. Of various sizes, subjects, and quality, but always watercolour. A few took pride of place in our homes, frequently adorning the same type of space/ allocated rooms as we relocated. *The Ancient Pine Root*, for example, always found its home above my father's large desk. My favourite has always been *Flowers in an Iron Pot*, which wasn't always on display, but when it was, was usually found near the dining room. A place of honour, really.

Traveling for the holidays, Grandfather's paintings, viewable in relatives houses, became a reference point and a way to understand my Grandfather. His body of work played on similar themes, and circled a familiar visual language stylistically. Even more, his scenes, and by extension his experiences, from Saugatuck, Vero Beach, Lafayette, etc. are therefore intimately connected with being a Ricks. Now, seeing them all together for the first time has also served importantly autobiographically. Telling the stories of past holiday travel and family rituals that formed the generation before me.

All signed, and one signed twice.

Jim Ricks
Dublin, Ireland
Autumn 2014

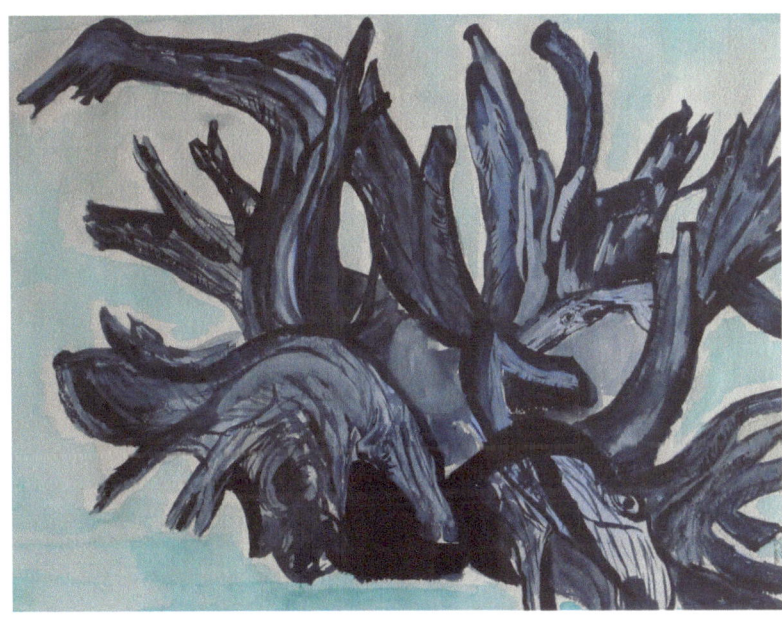

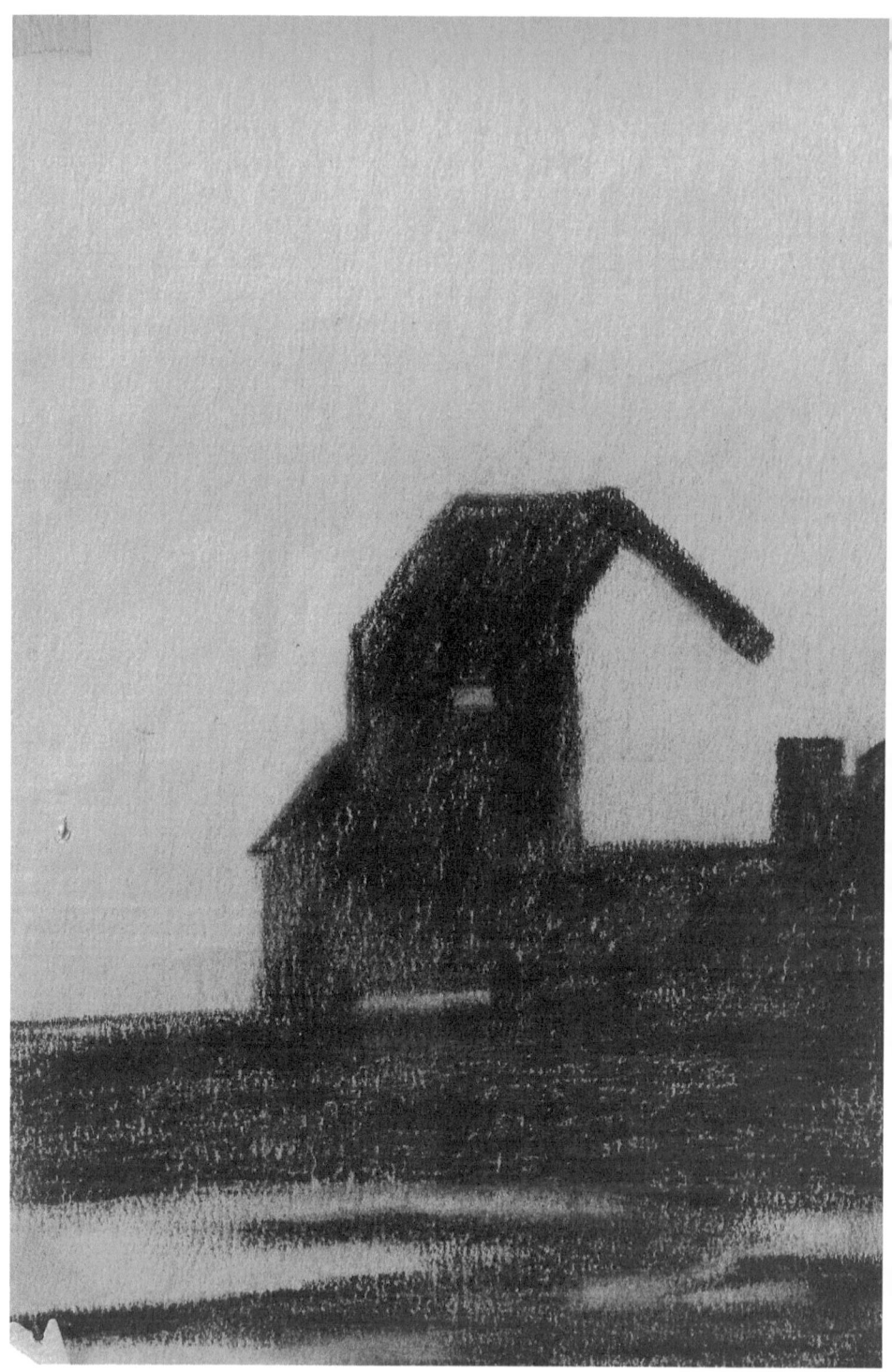

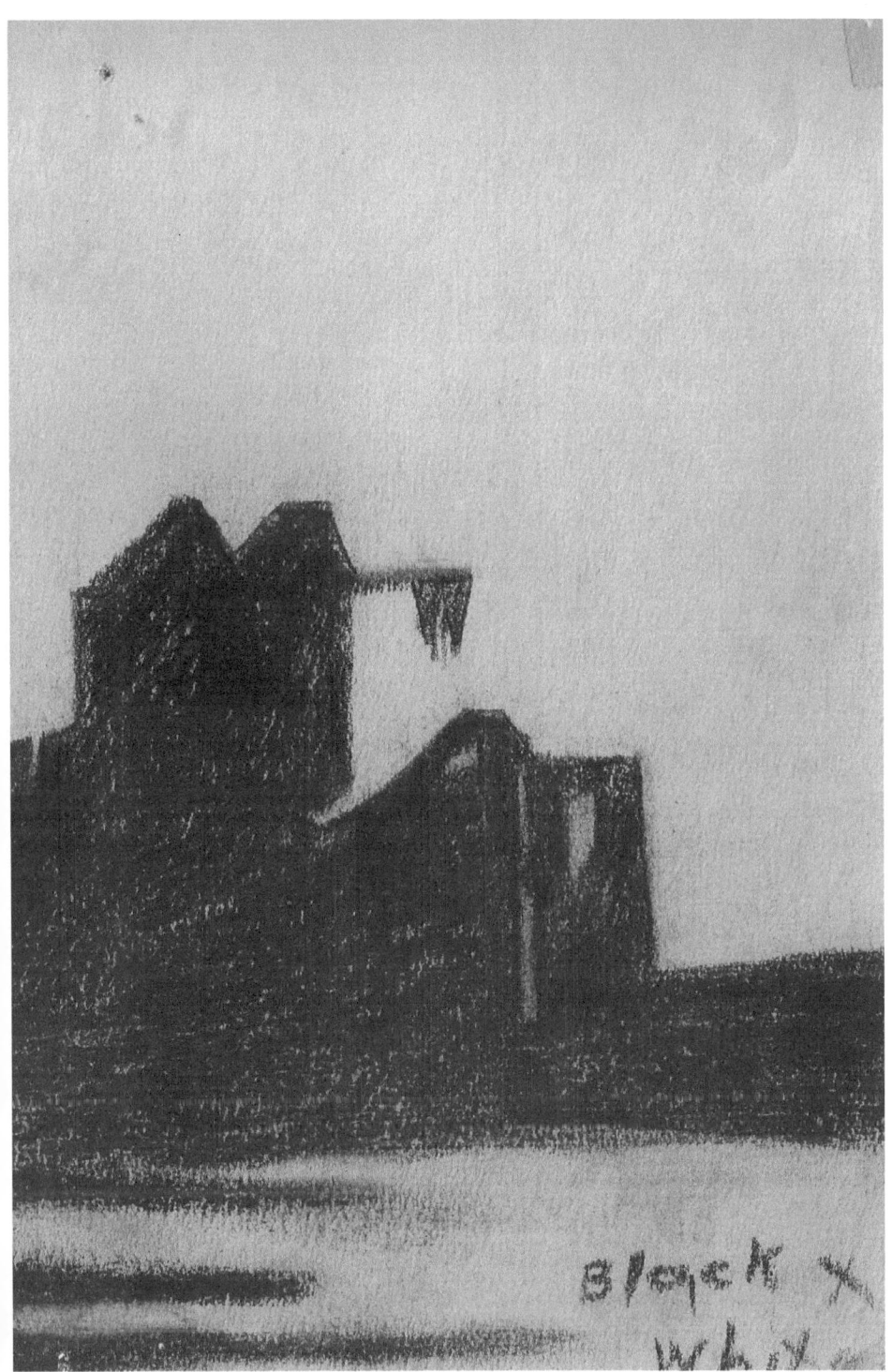

Black x
White

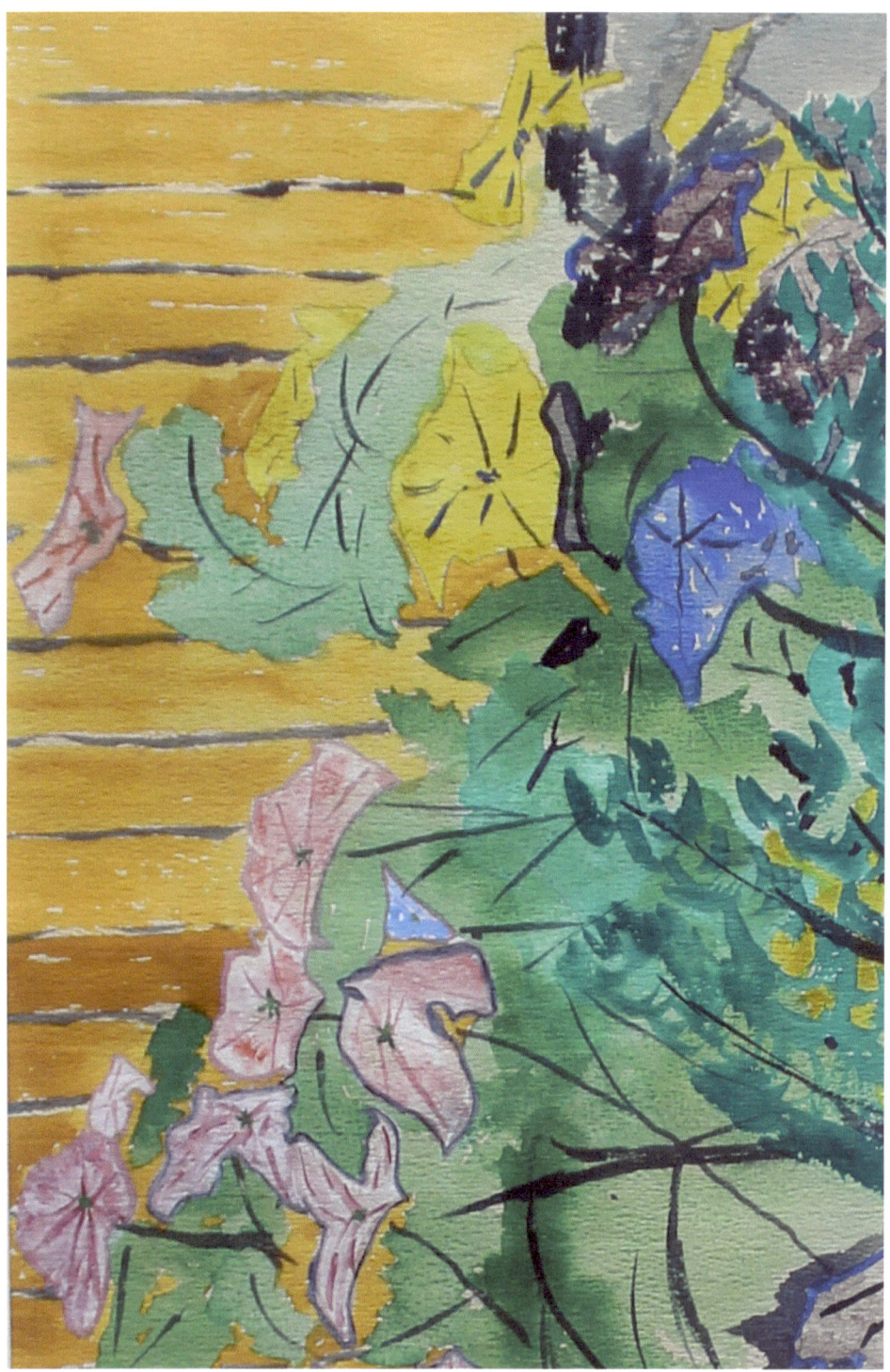

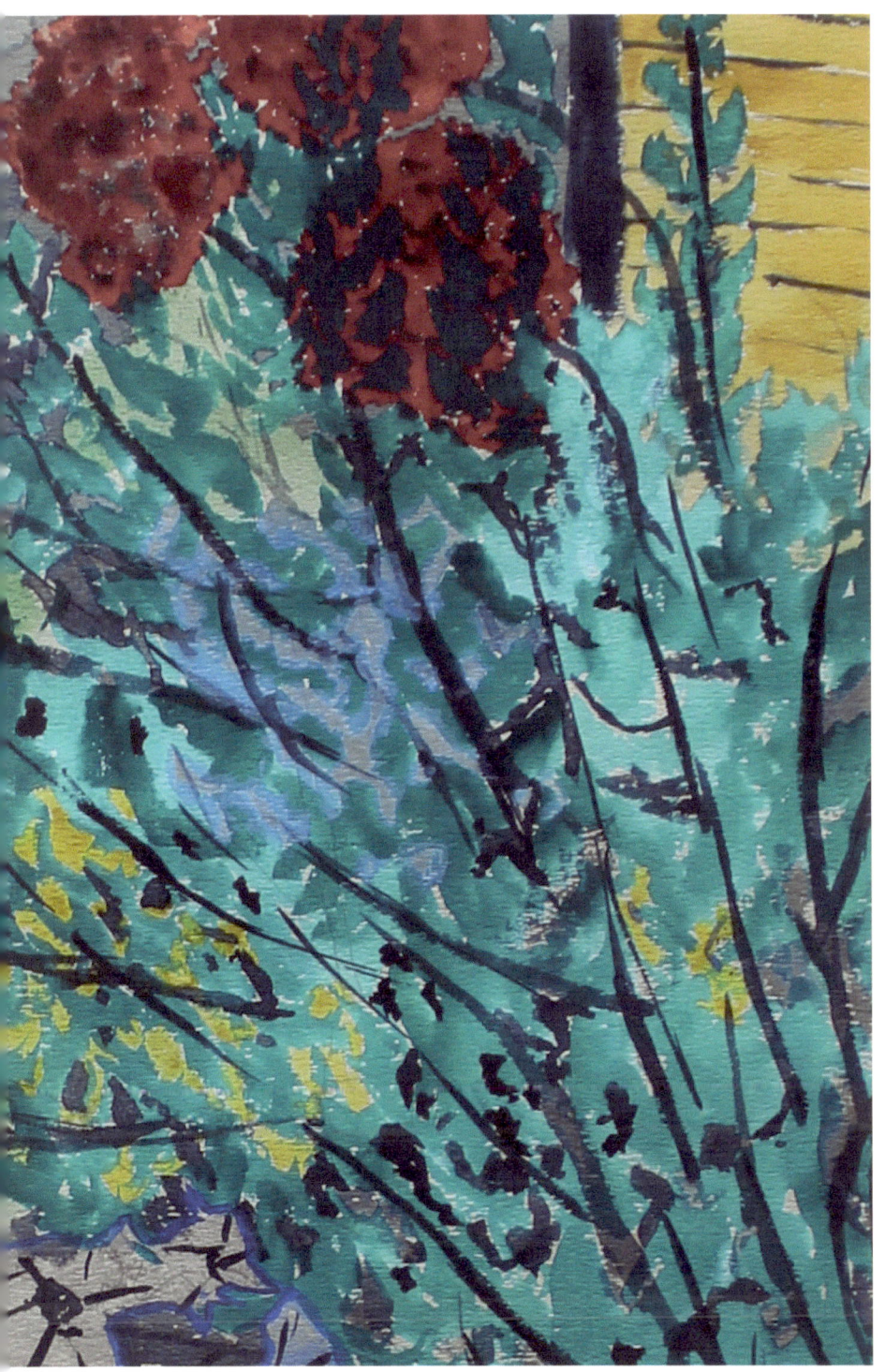

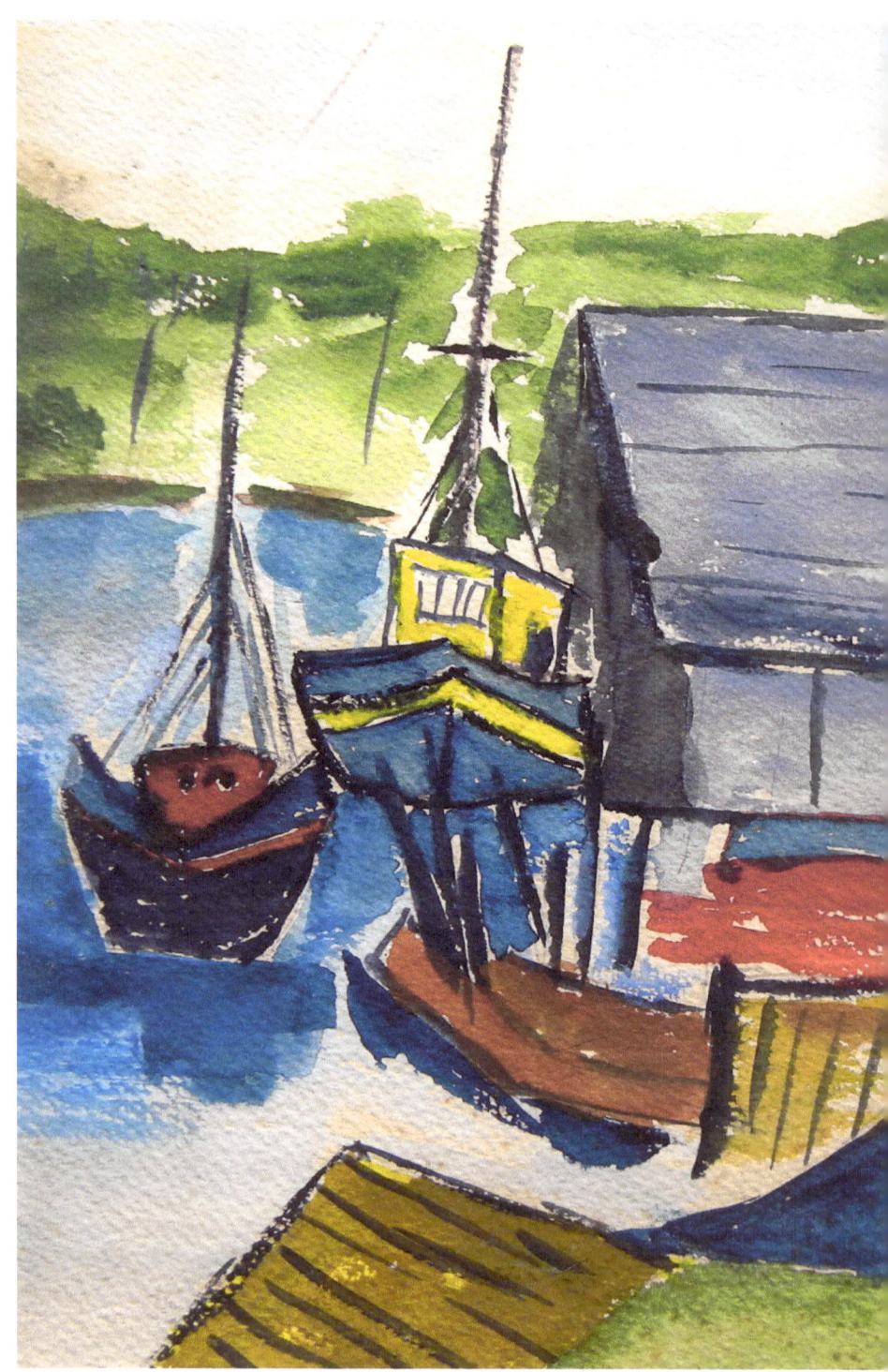

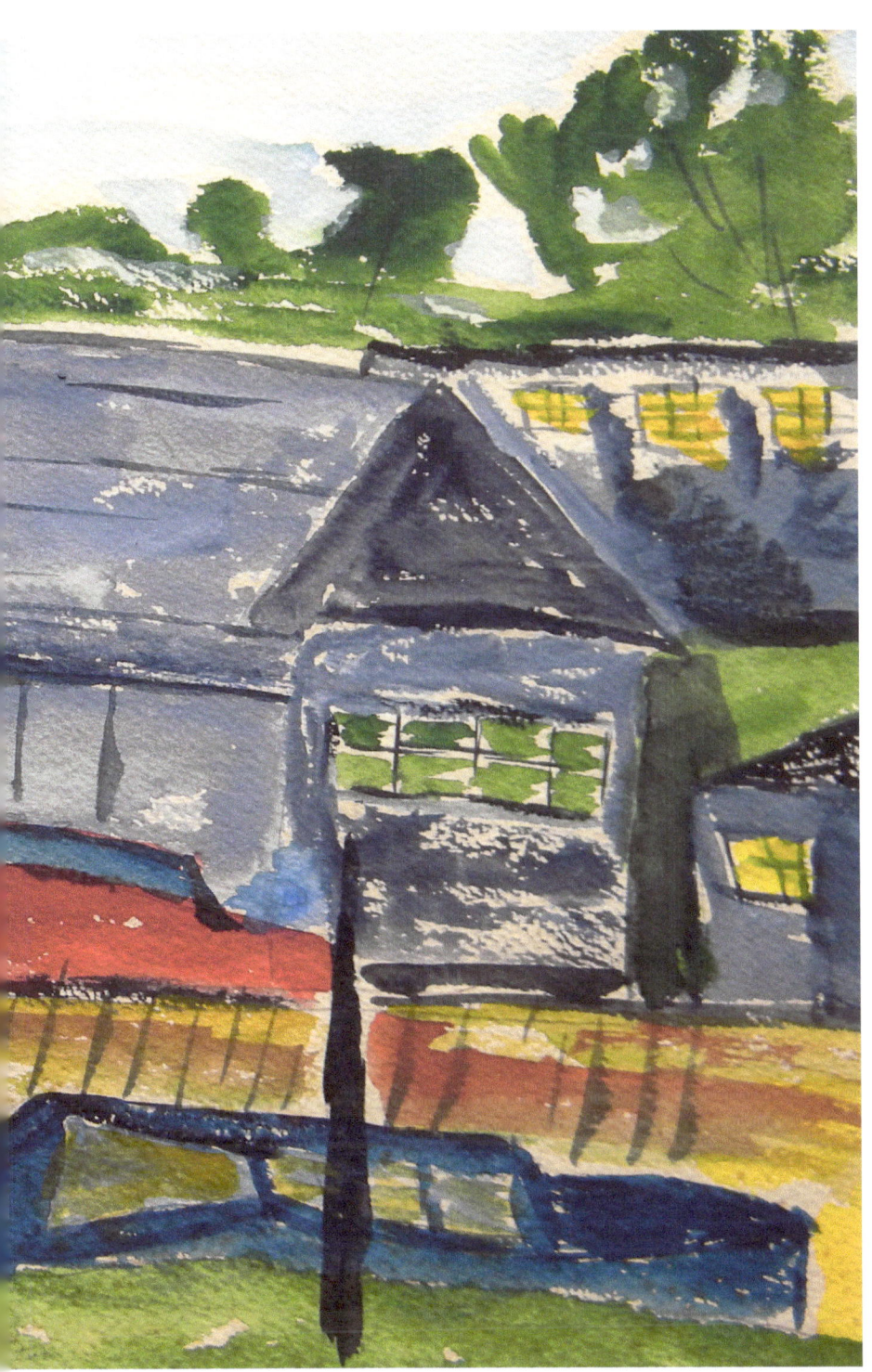

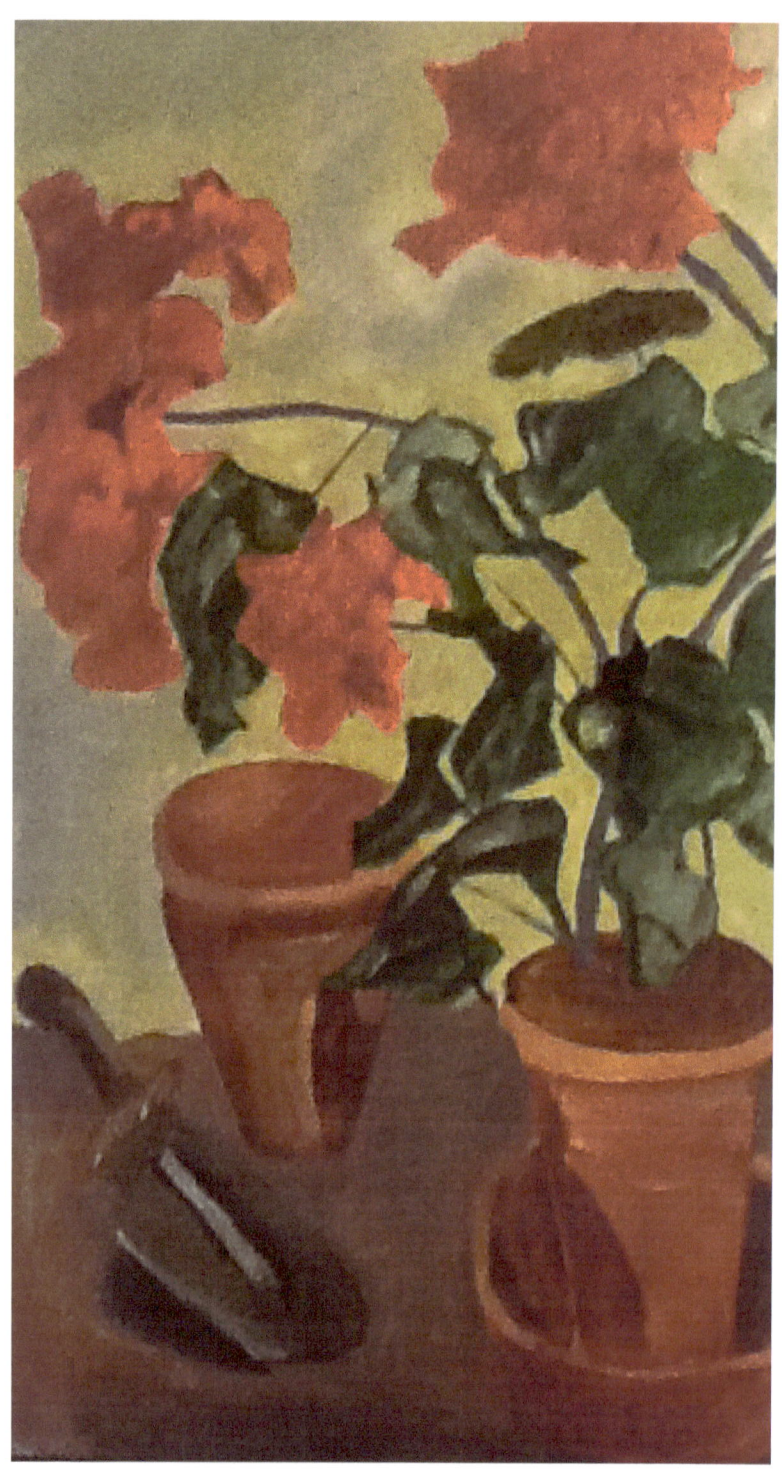

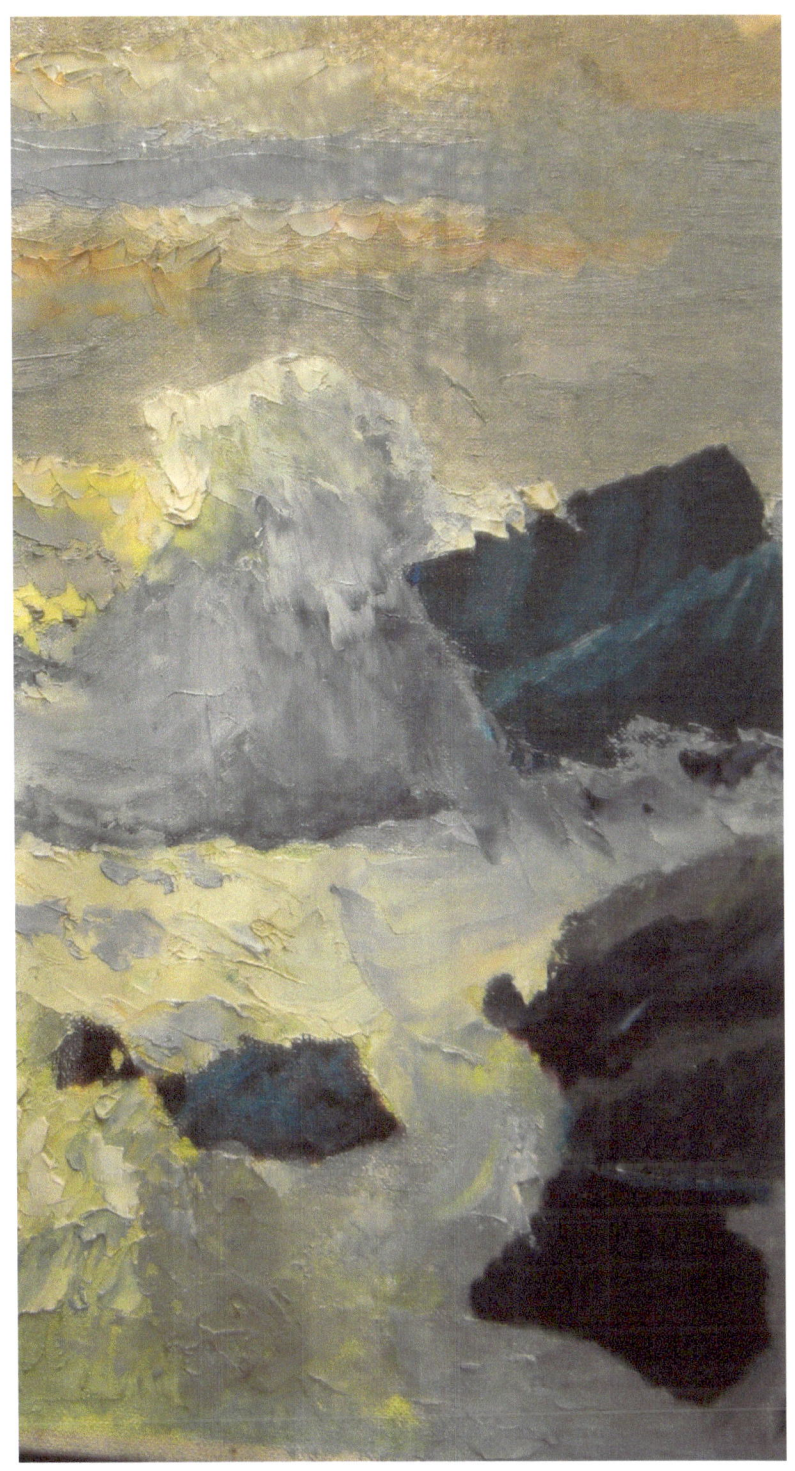

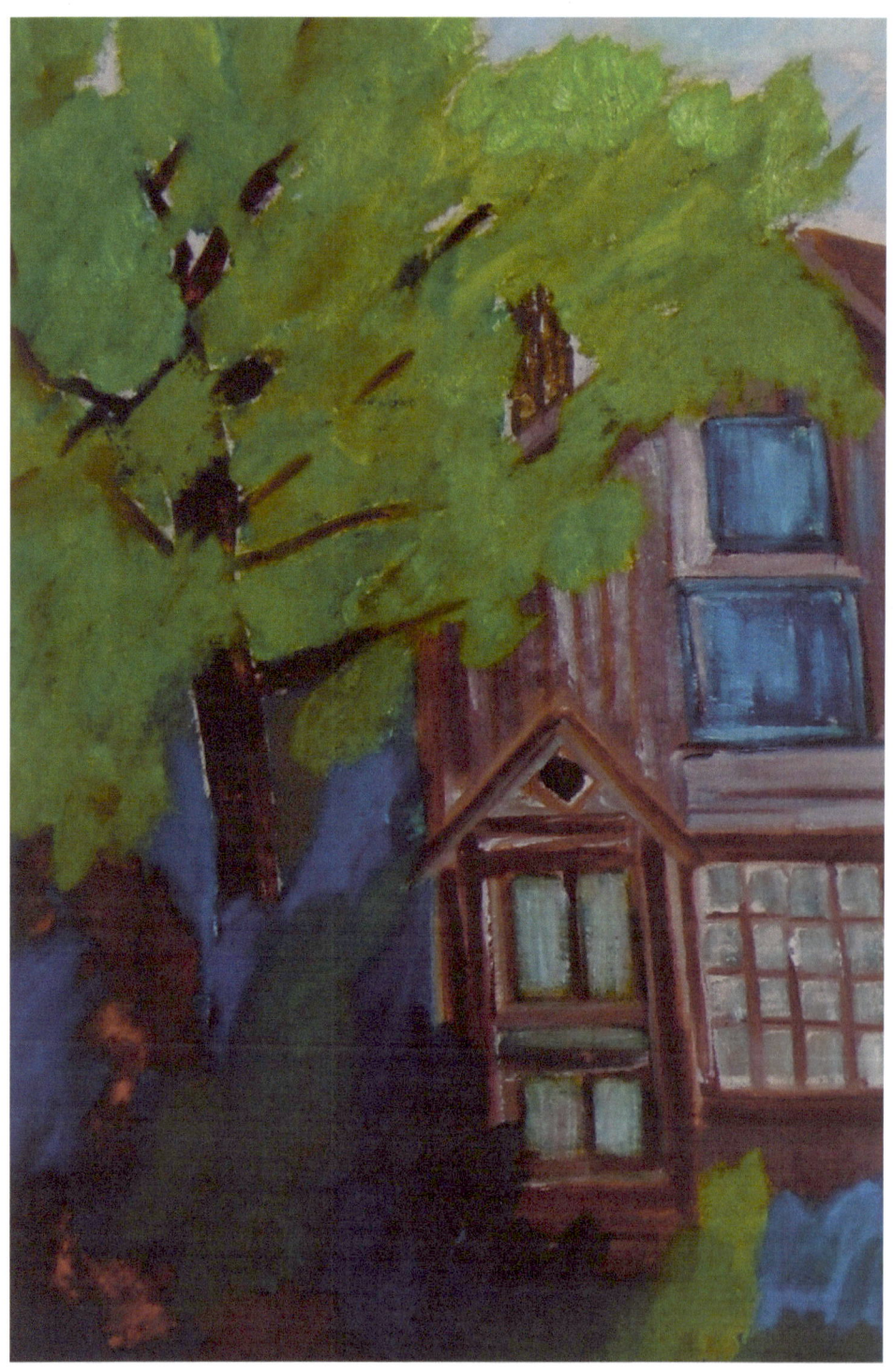

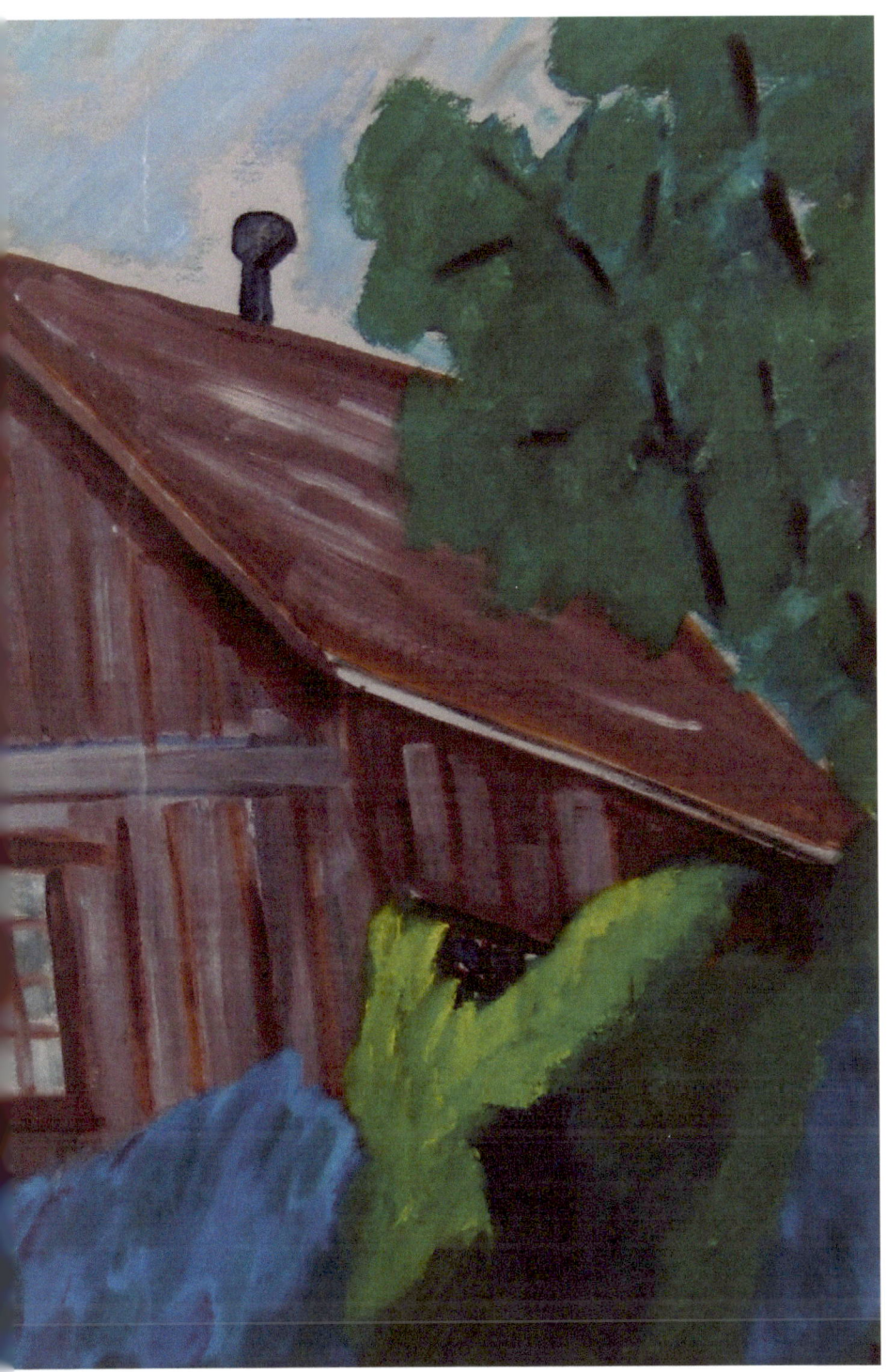

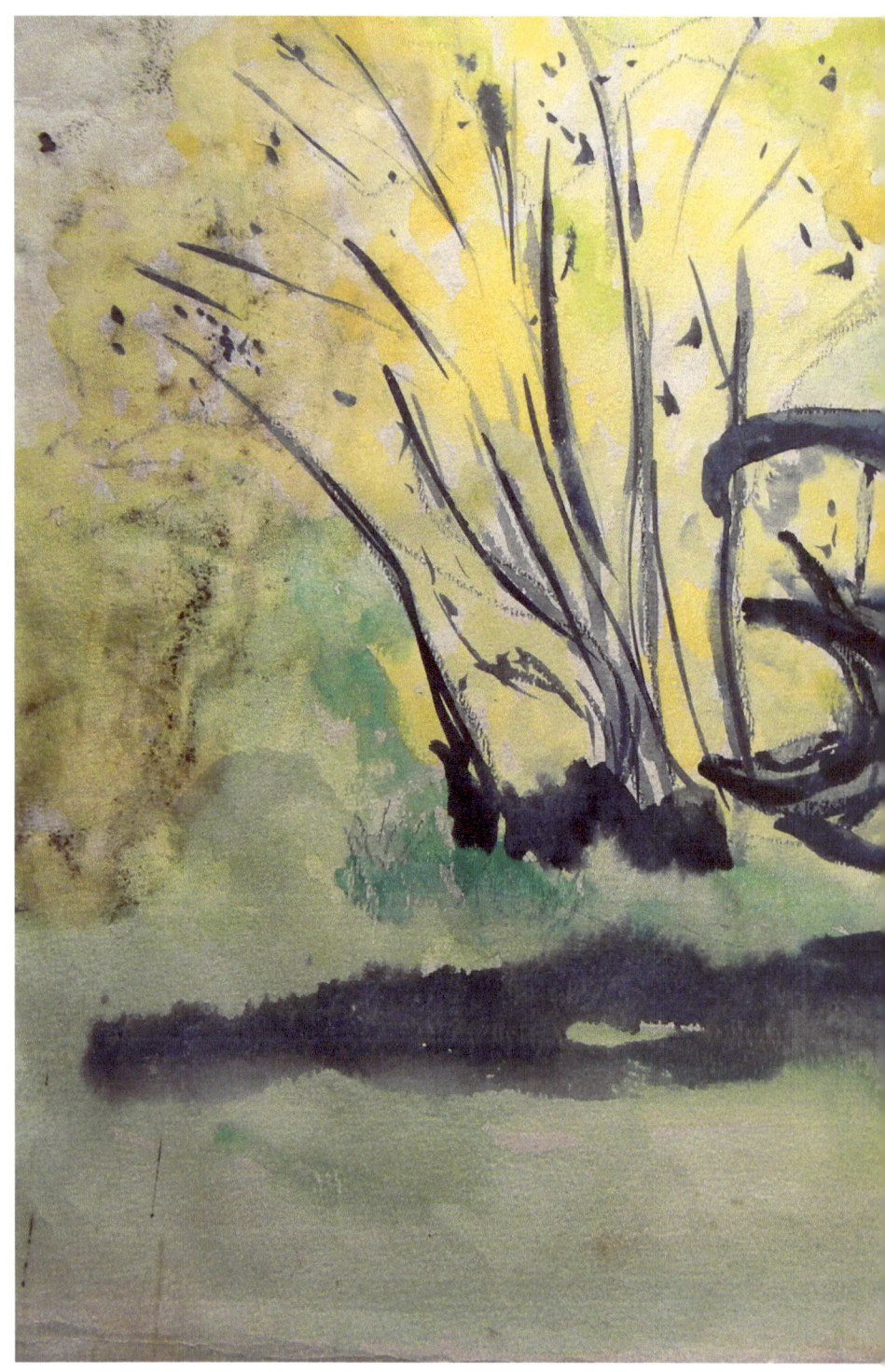

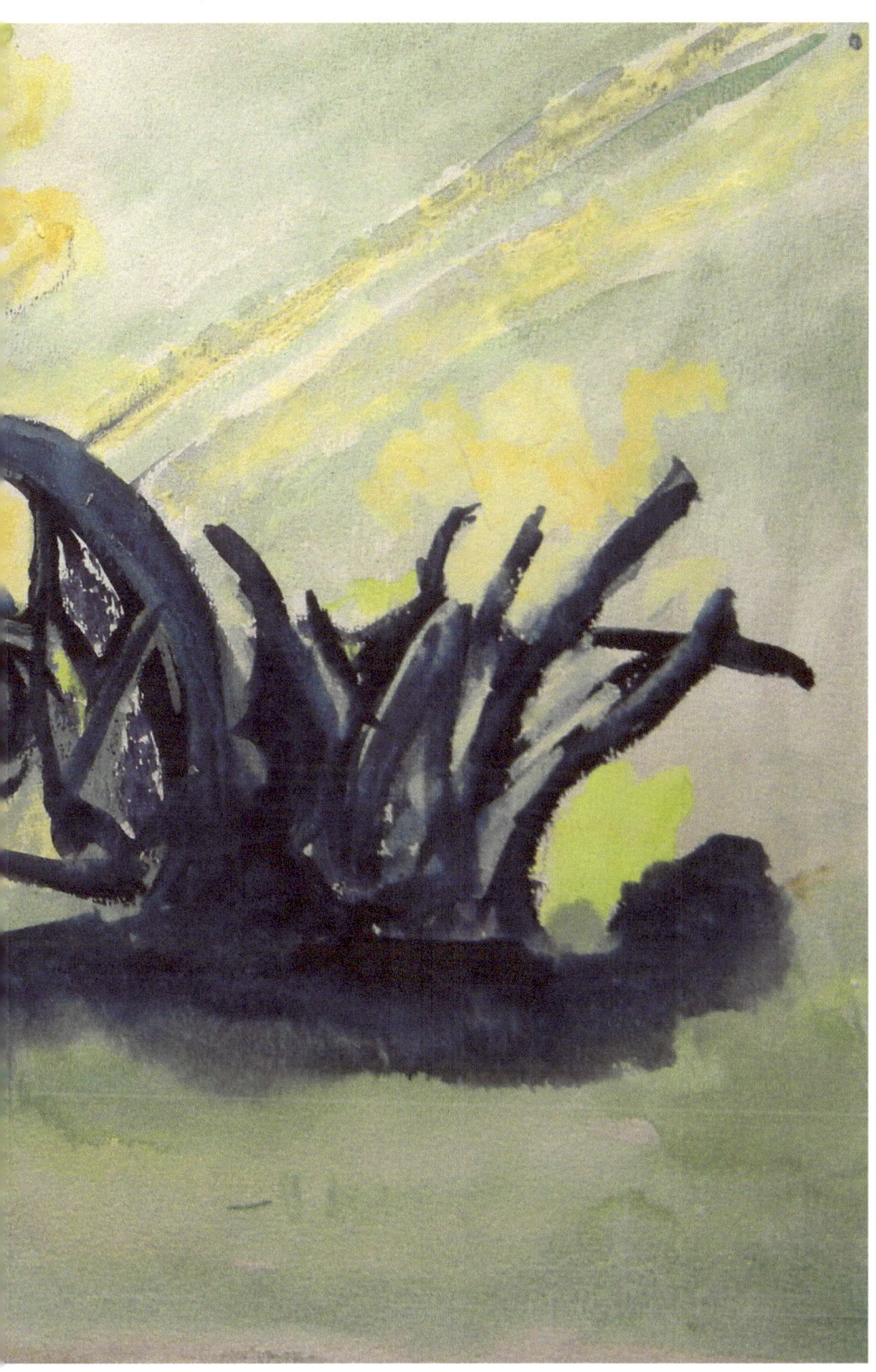

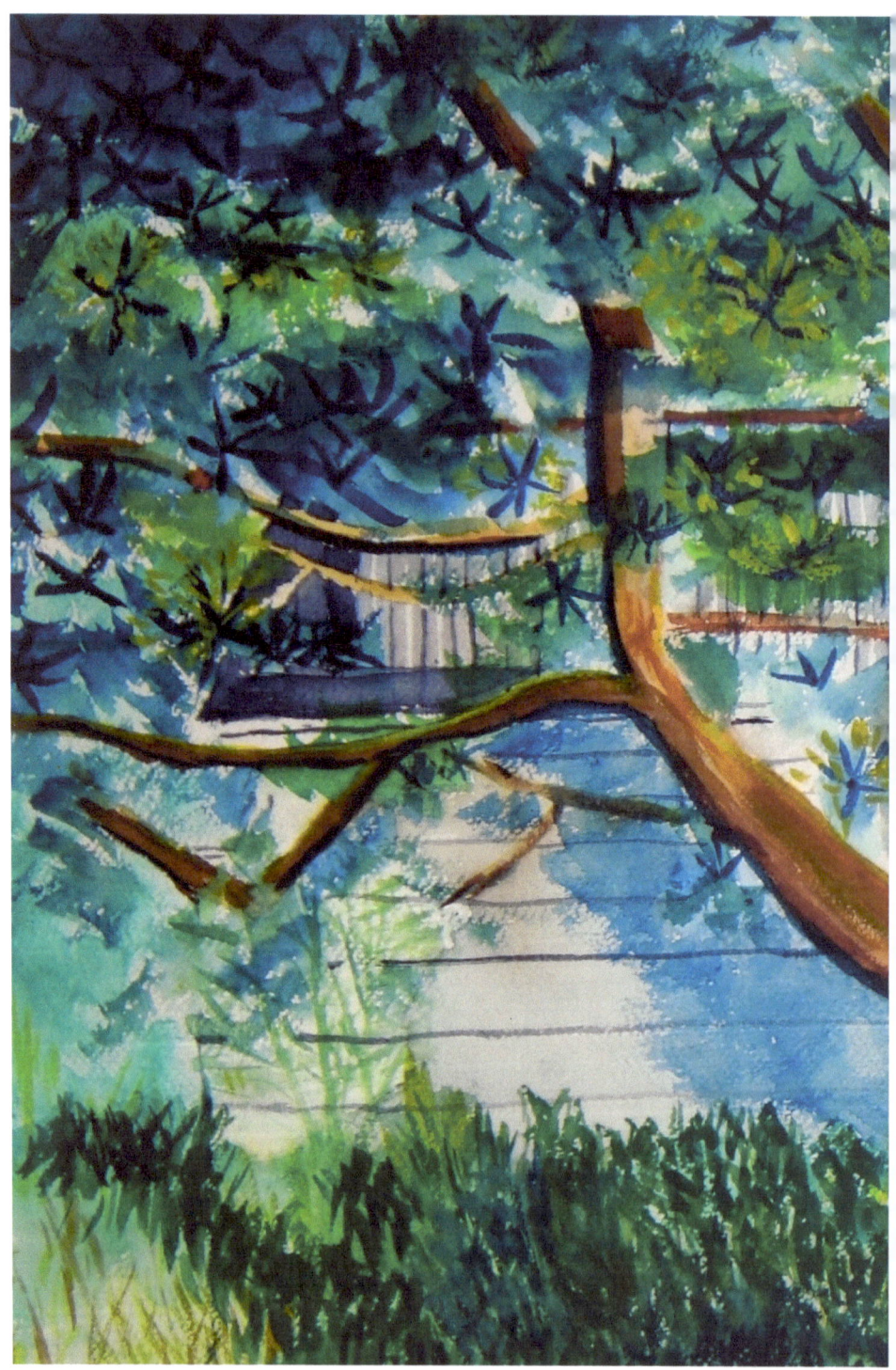

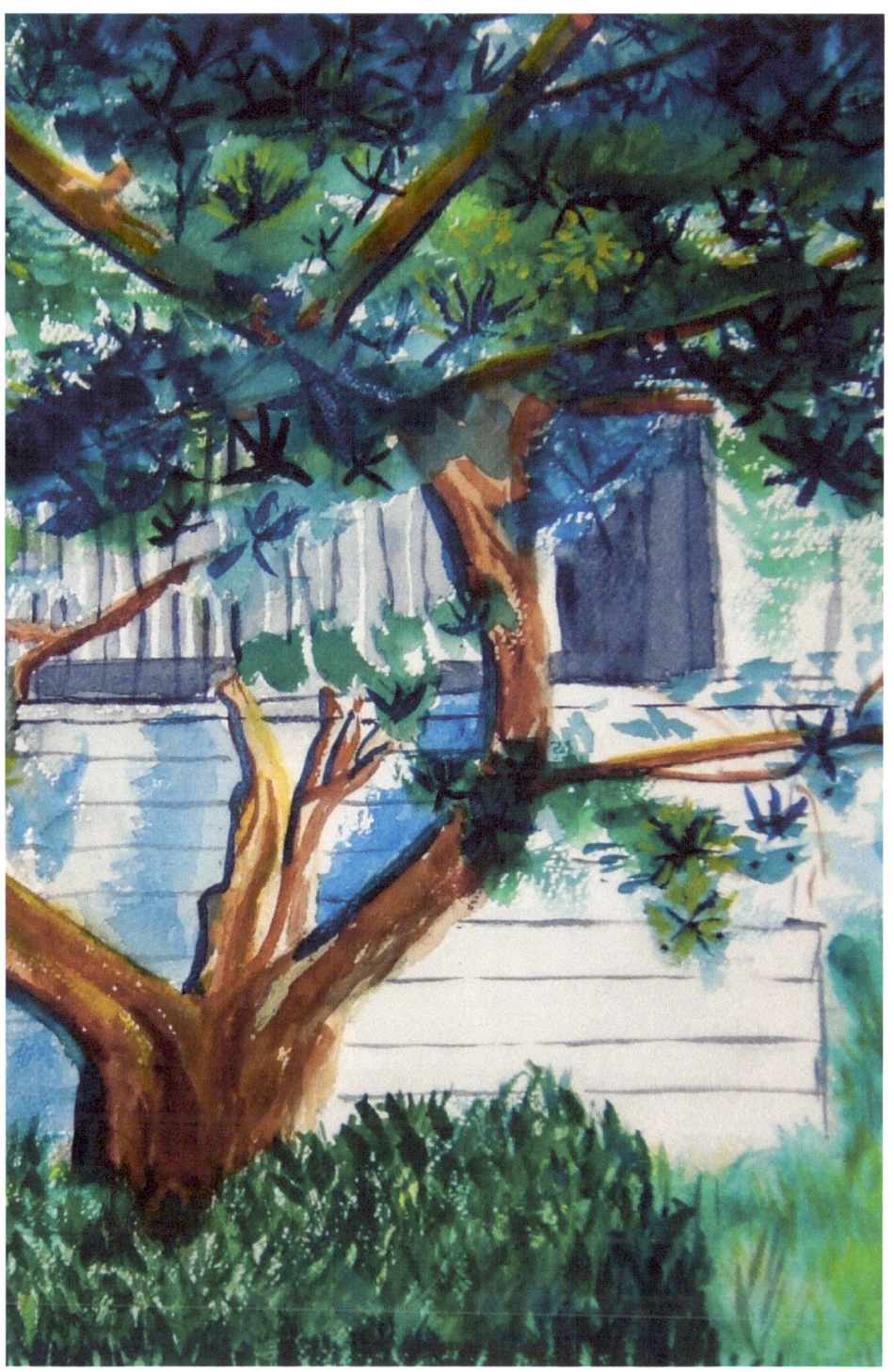

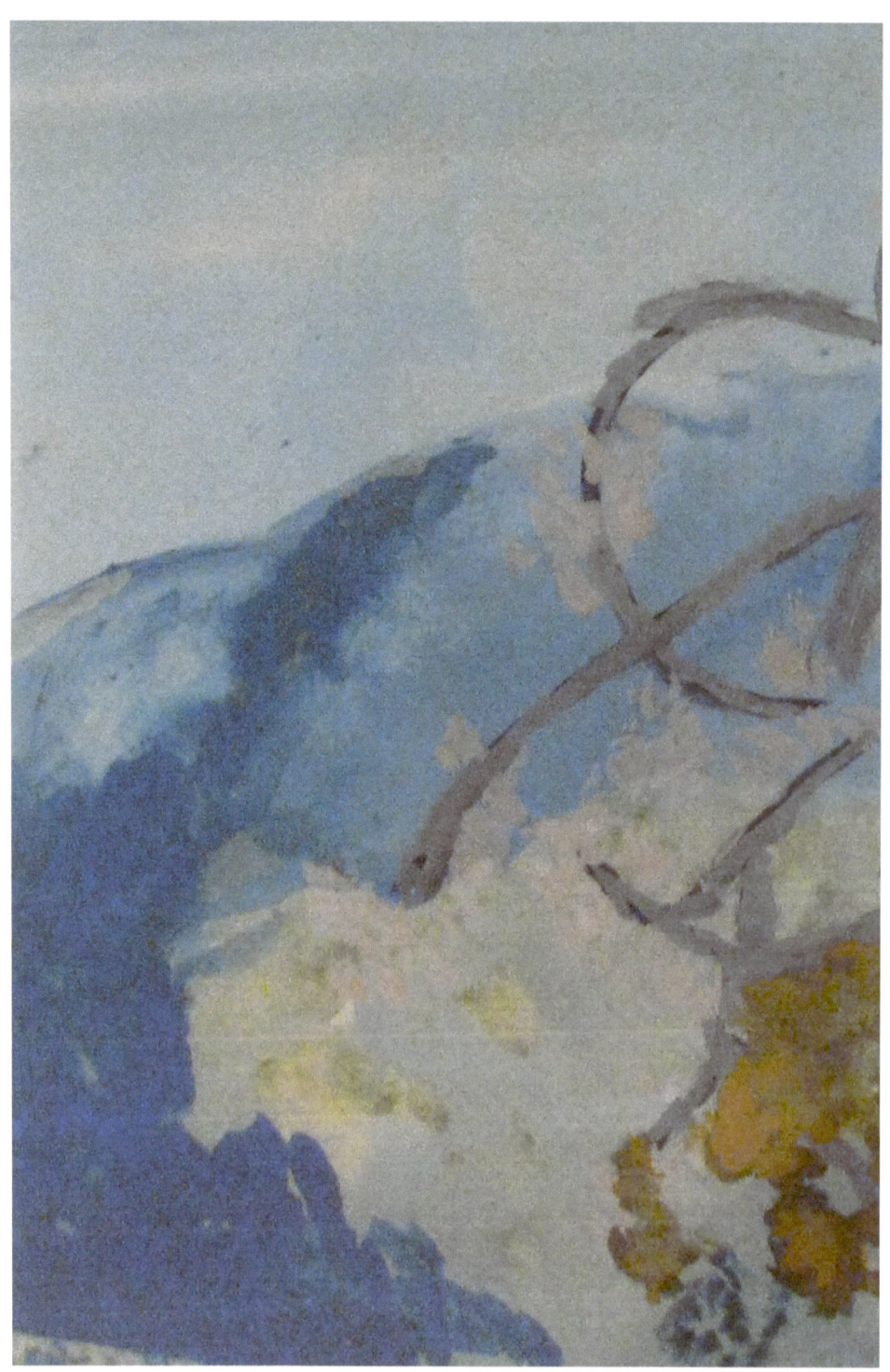

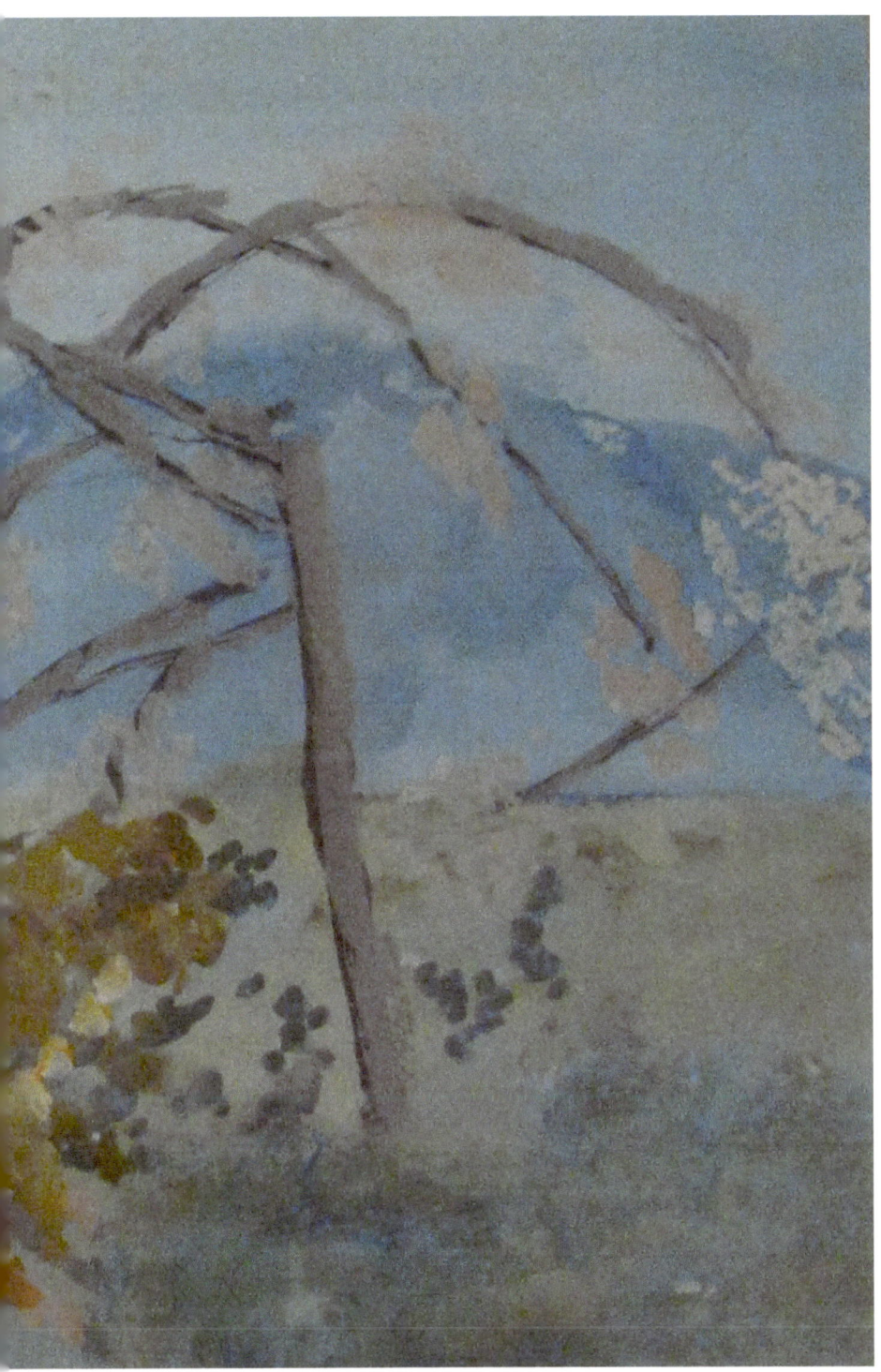

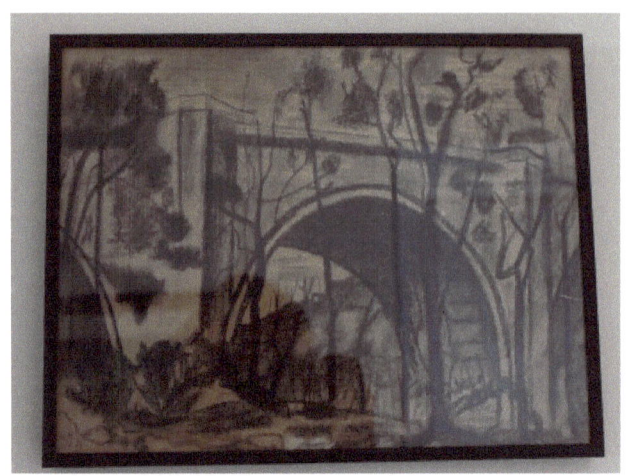

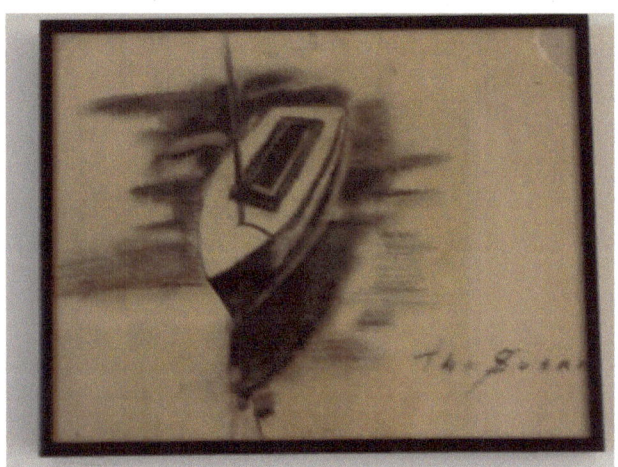

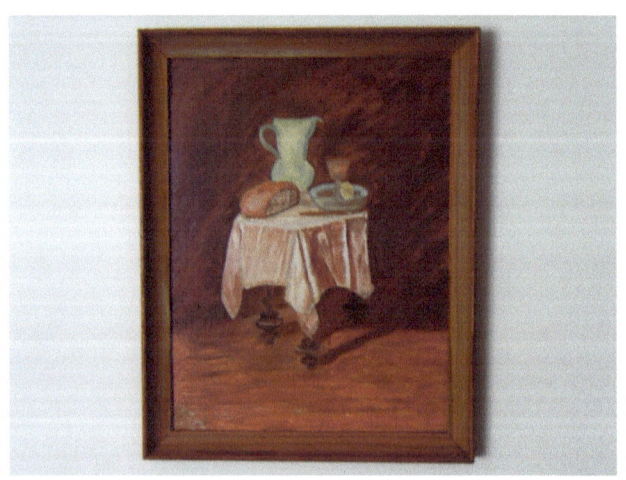

The Rock Creek Bridge
1950's
Charcoal
12" x 8"
Collection of Suzi R. and John V. Austin

The Susan
1950's
Charcoal
12" x 8"
Collection of Suzi R. and John V. Austin

Solitary Meal
1957
Oil
16" x 20"
Collection of Alan E. and Barbara G. Ricks

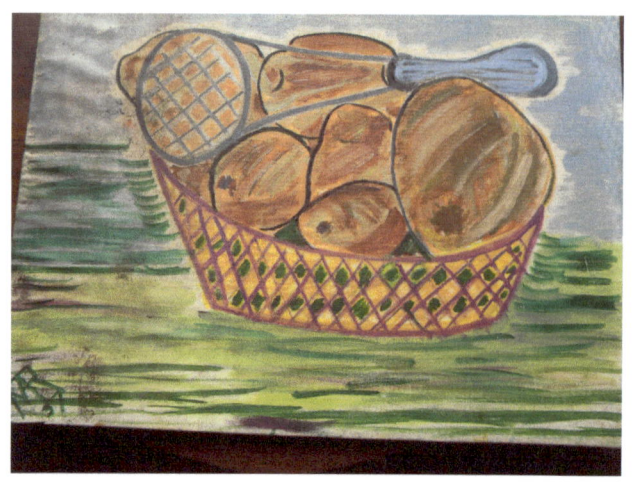

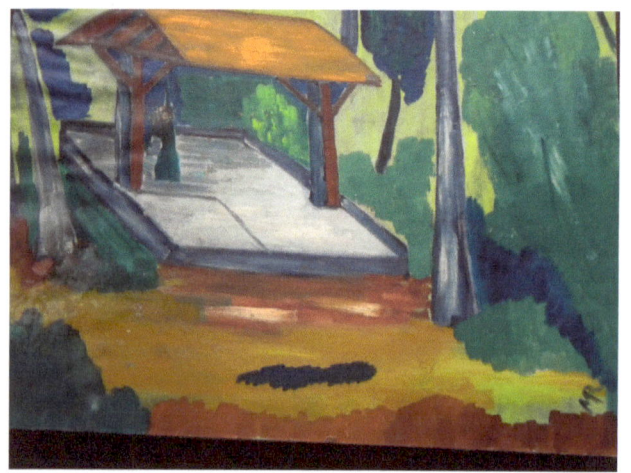

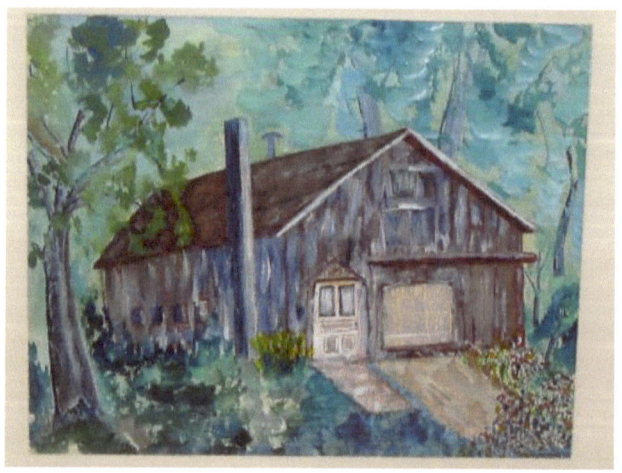

The Potato Basket
1957
Acrylic on art board
20" x 16"
Collection of Michael J. and Susan L. Ricks

Well House
1960
Oil on art board
28" x 20"
Collection of Michael J. and Susan L. Ricks

Carl Byrd's Cabin
1960
Oil
29 1/2" x 24 1/2"
Collection of Suzi R. and John V. Austin

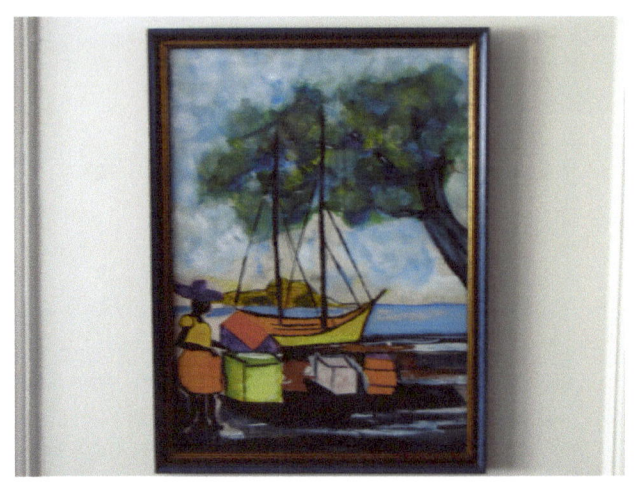

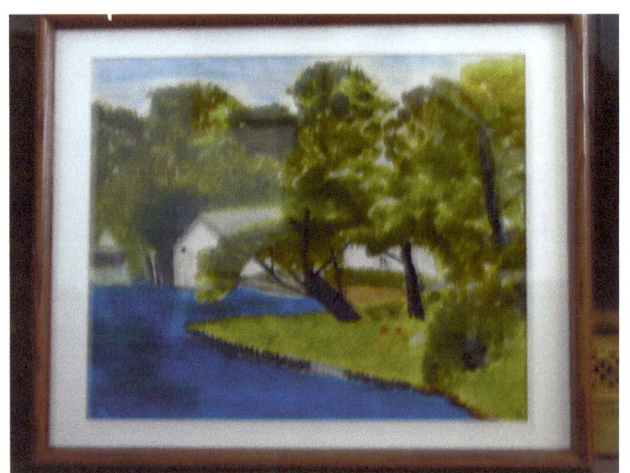

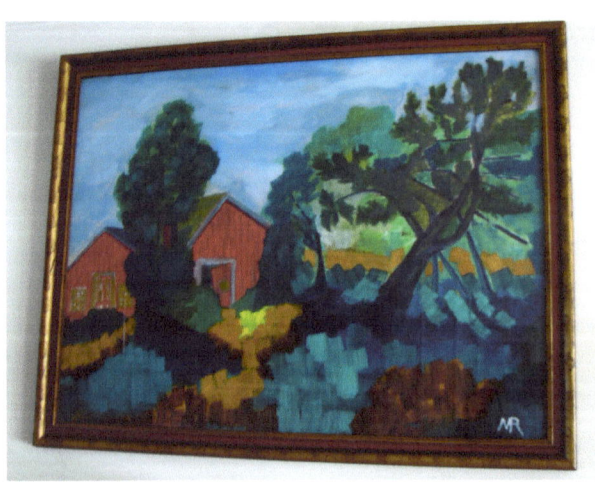

Woman with Boat
1960
Watercolor
12" x 16"
Collection of Thomas M. and Janice D. Ricks

Kalamazoo River Canal with Trees
1960
Watercolor
21" x 17"
Collection of Thomas M. and Janice D. Ricks

The Oxbow Club and Tree
1960
Oil
28" x 20"
Collection of Stephen A. and Diana M. Ricks

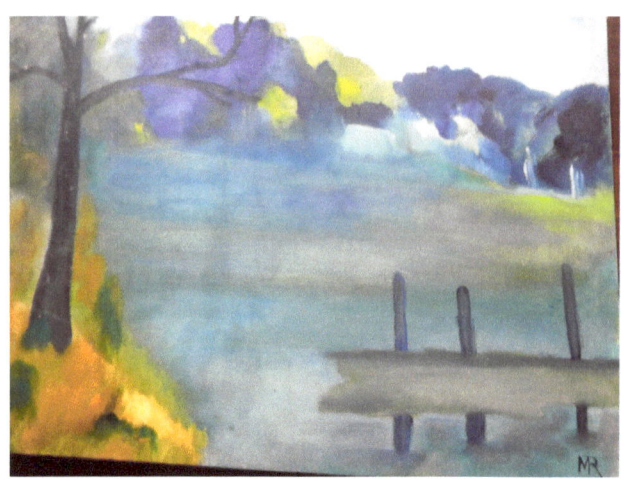

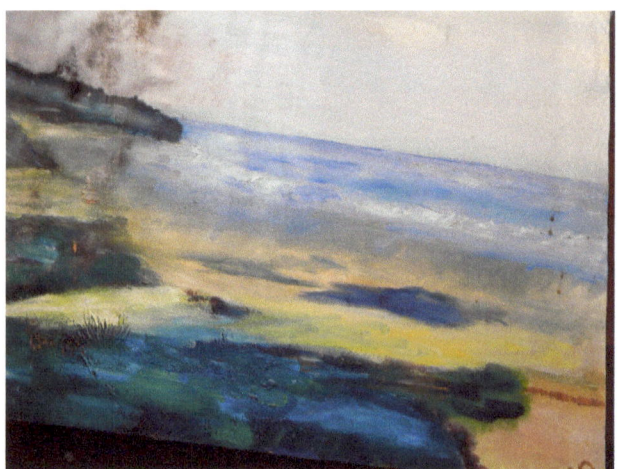

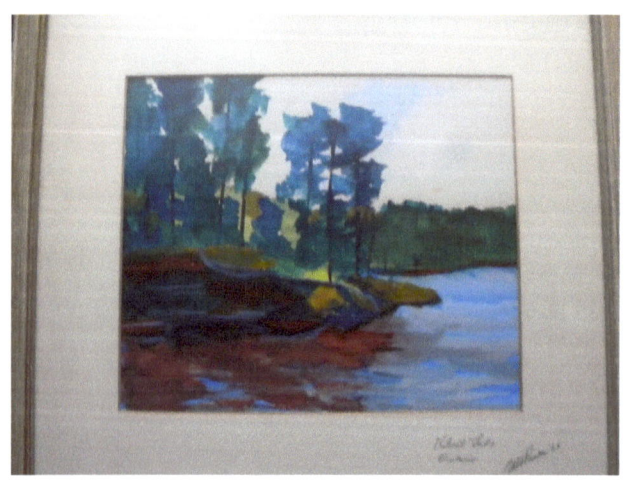

Pine (Unfinished)
N/A
Watercolor on paper
24" x 18"
Collection of Michael J. and Susan L. Ricks

Lake Michigan Shore
1960
Oil on art board
24" x 18"
Collection of Michael J. and Susan L. Ricks

Kilvert Lake
1960
Oil
30" x 24"
Collection of Michael J. and Susan L. Ricks

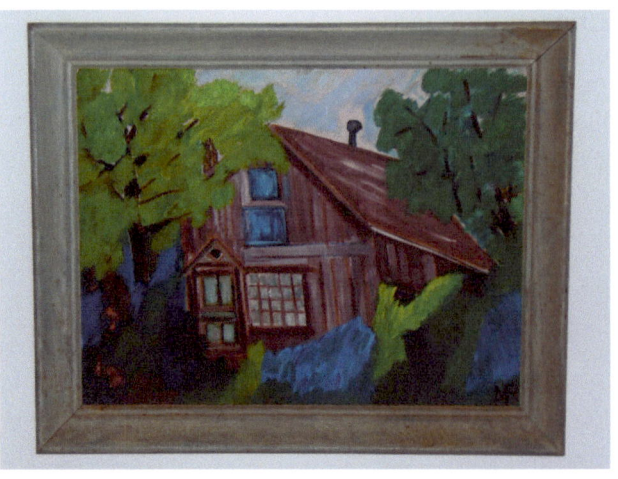

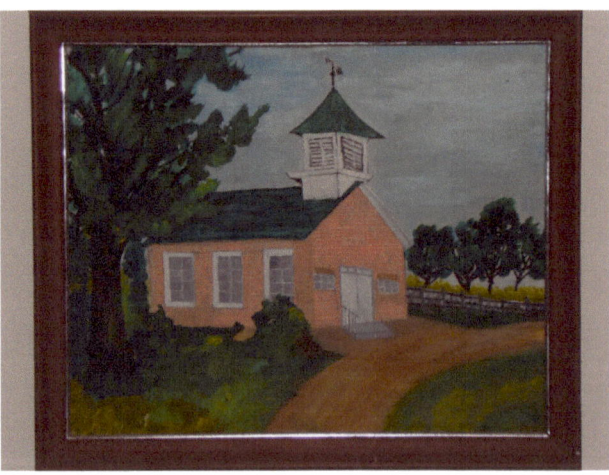

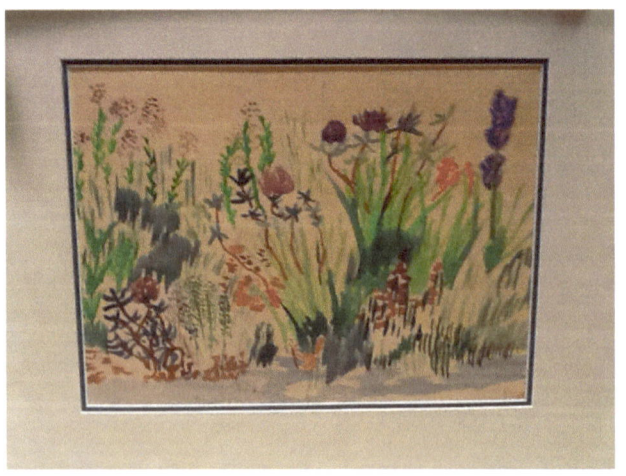

First Cottage
1960's
Oil
28" x 22"
Collection of Alan E. and Barbara G. Ricks

One Room Schoolhouse
1960's
Oil
22 1/2" x 18 1/4"
Collection of Alan E. and Barbara G. Ricks

Wildflowers
1960's
Watercolor
19" x 16"
Collection of Laura B. Austin

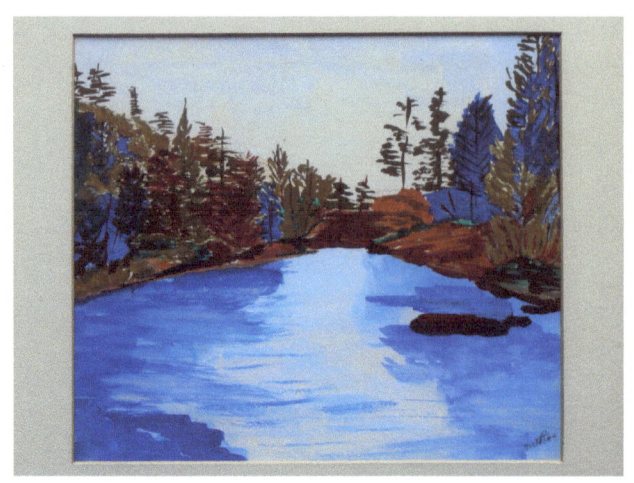

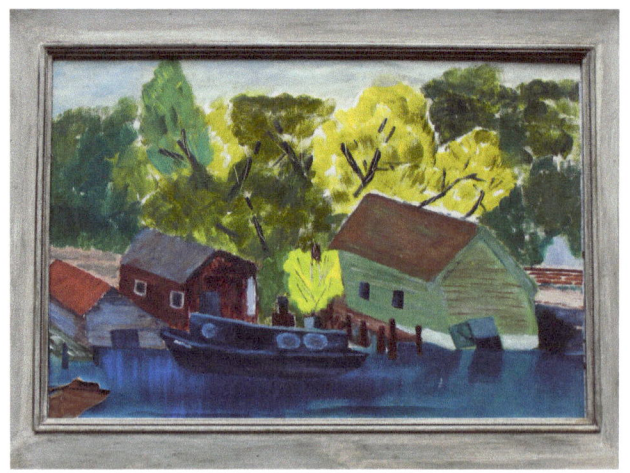

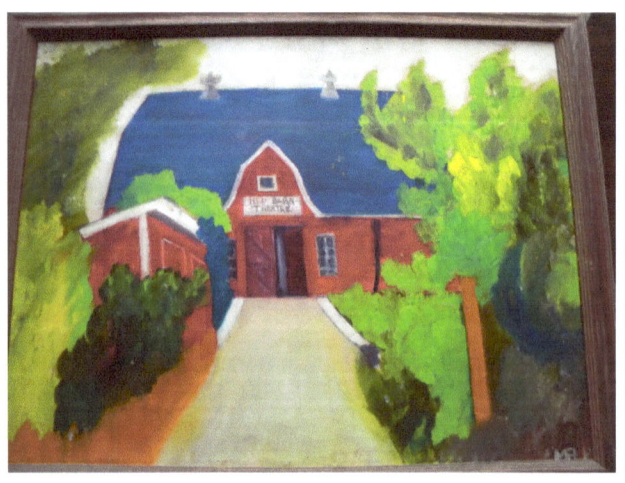

Dogtooth Lake
1960
Watercolor
15 1⁄4" x 14"
Collection of Theodore C. and Margaret B.
Ricks

Fish Wharf
1960
Oil on board
21 1⁄2" x 13 3⁄4"
Collection of Theodore C. and Margaret B.
Ricks

Red Barn
1961
Oil
23" x 16"
Collection of Michael J. and Susan L. Ricks

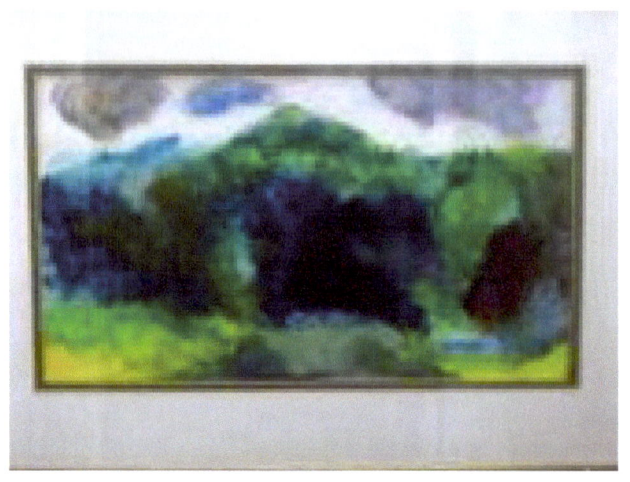

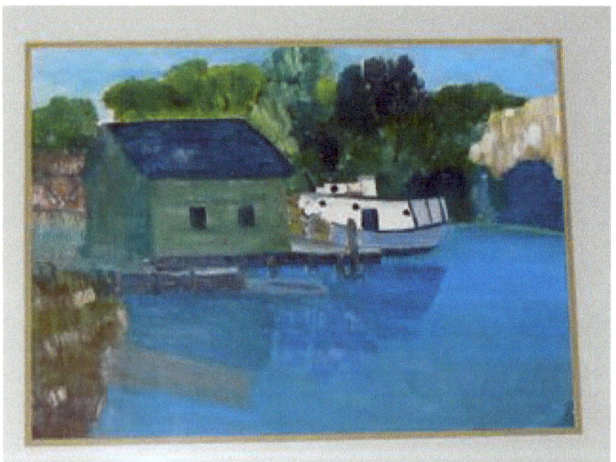

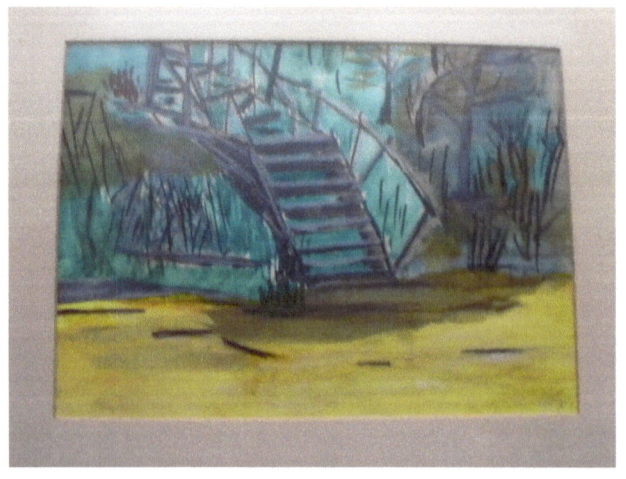

Mountain Abstract
Summer 1964
Watercolor
24 1/2" x 19"
Collection of Stephen A. and Diana M. Ricks

*Exhibited at the Central Illinois Art Exhibit Decatur, IL March 7-28, 1965

Kalamazoo River
1964
Watercolor
24 1/2" x 19"
Collection of Suzi R. and John V. Austin

Steps to Lake Michigan Beach
1964
Oil
16" x 12"
Collection of Michael J. and Susan L. Ricks

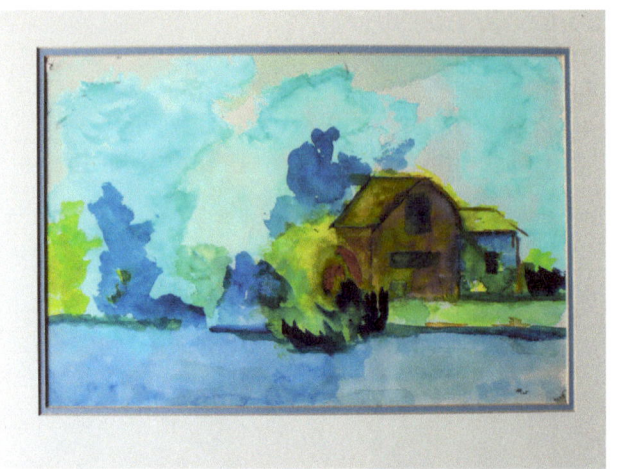

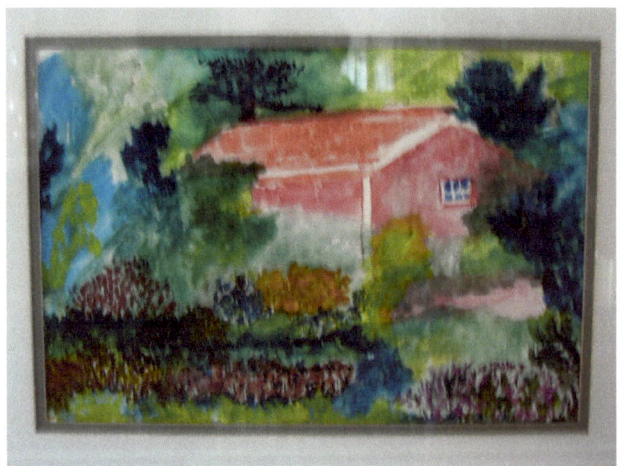

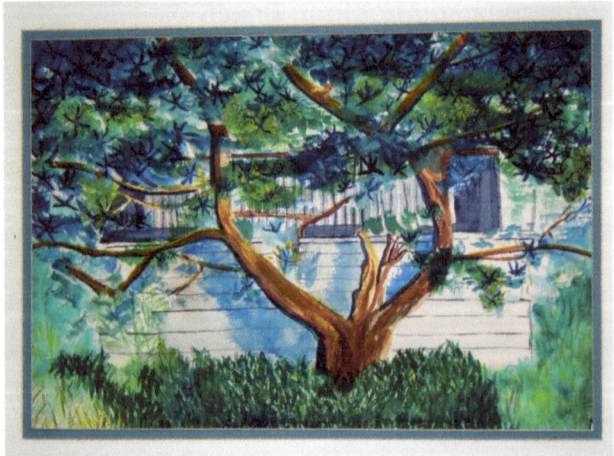

Mill on the Saugatuck River, MI
1965
Watercolor
25" x 19"
Collection of Theodore C. and Margaret B. Ricks

Van Syckle Garden
1966
Watercolor
18 1/2" x 12 1/2"
Collection of Stephen A. and Diana M. Ricks

Gallery at Oxbow
1966
Watercolor
28 1/2" x 22"
Collection of Alan E. and Barbara G. Ricks

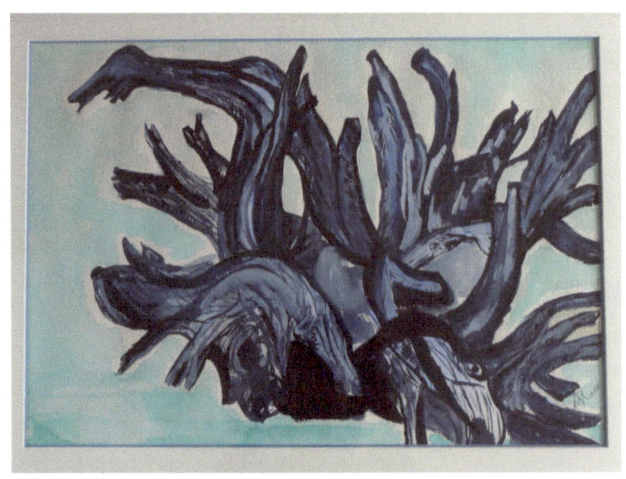

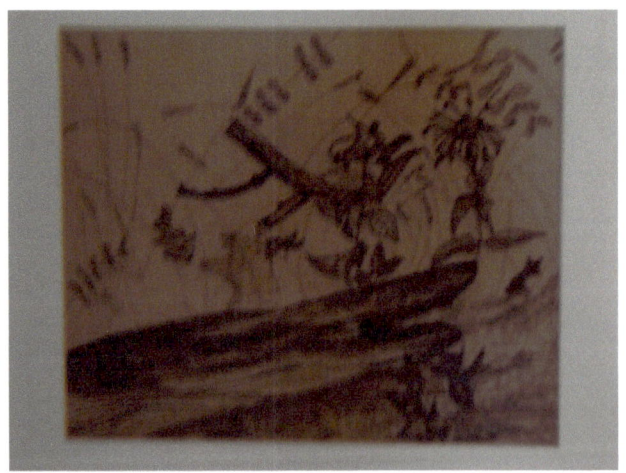

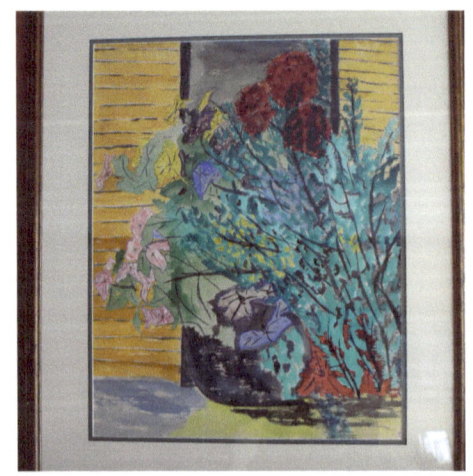

An Ancient Pine Root
Watercolor
30" x 23 3⁄4"
Collection of Theodore C. and Margaret B.
Ricks

*Hung in the Central Illinois Art Exhibit, Decatur, IL March 7-28, 1965 and won an honorable mention in the Lafayette Art Center on exhibition

Driftwood
1968
Watercolor
18" x 16 1⁄2"
Collection of Alan E. and Barbara G. Ricks

Flowers in an Iron Pot
1969
Watercolor
26 1⁄2" x 31 3⁄4"
Collection of Theodore C. and Margaret B.
Ricks

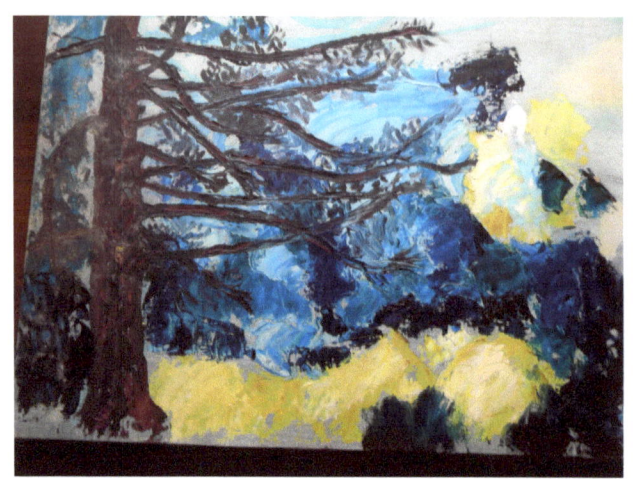

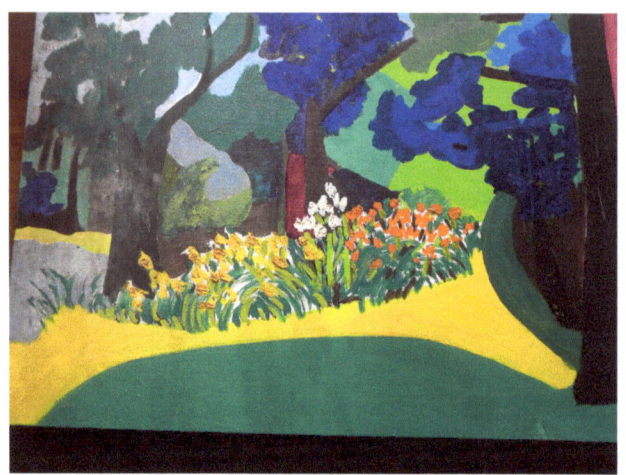

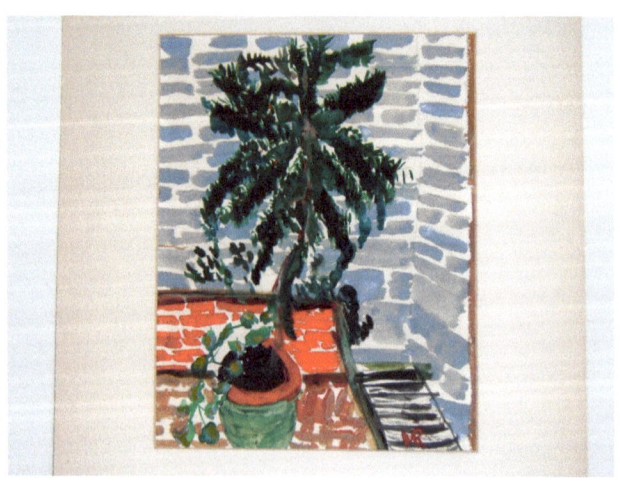

Pine Tree
1971
Oil on art board
24" x 18"
Collection of Michael J. and Susan L. Ricks

Garden
N/A
Oil on art board
24" x 18"
Collection of Michael J. and Susan L. Ricks

Norfolk Pine on Patio
1974
Watercolor
13" x 16" (unframed)
Collection of Alan E. and Barbara C. Ricks

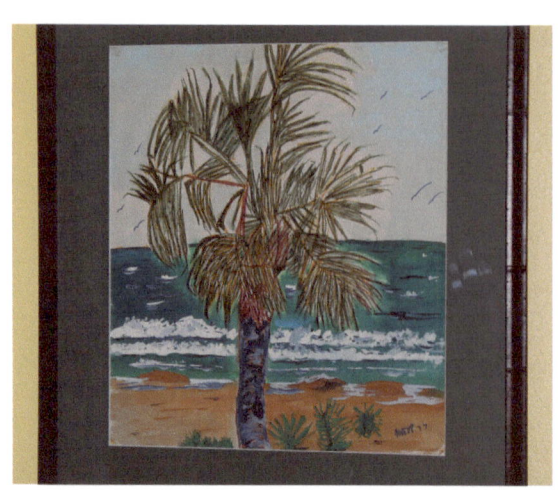

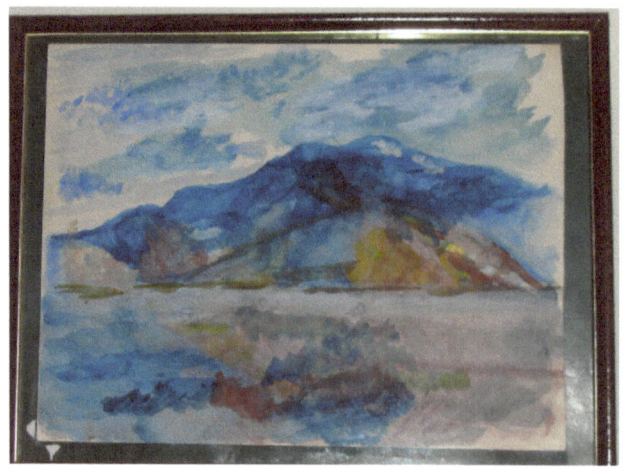

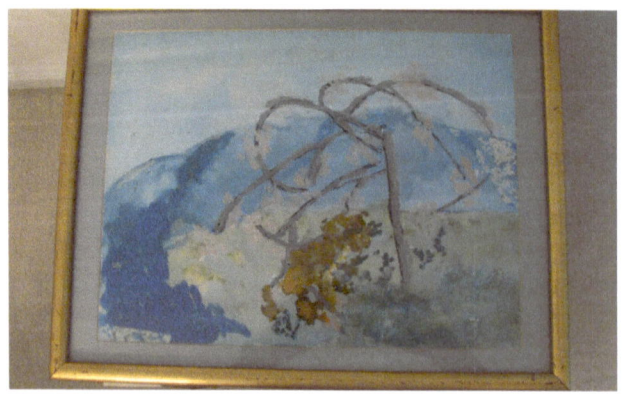

Palm Tree
1977
Watercolor
13 6/8" x 15 7/8"
Collection of Theodore C. and Margaret B.
Ricks

Sangre de Christo Mountains
July 1984
Watercolor
16 3/4" x 12 3/4"
Collection of Thomas M. and Janice D. Ricks

Floral Landscape (practice)
N/A
Watercolor
10 1/2" x 15 1/2"
Collection of Thomas M. and Janice D. Ricks

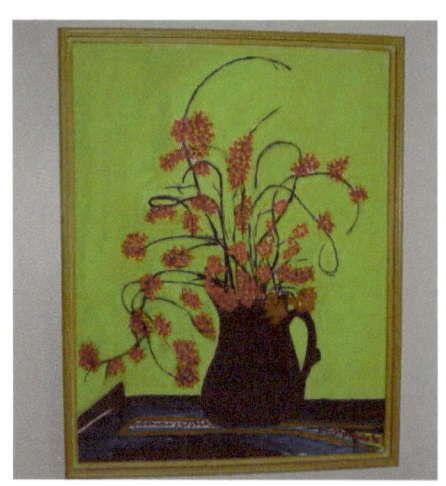

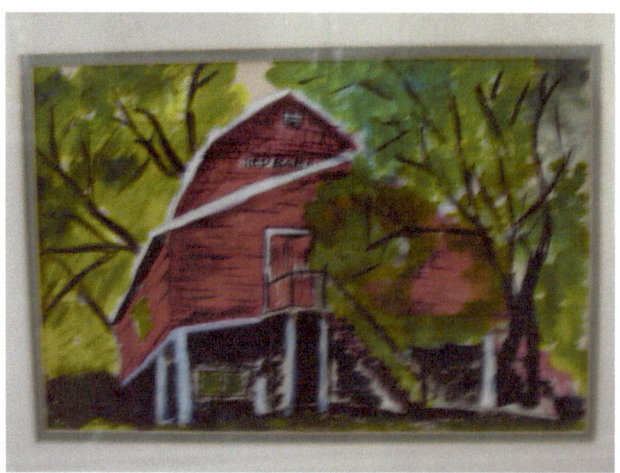

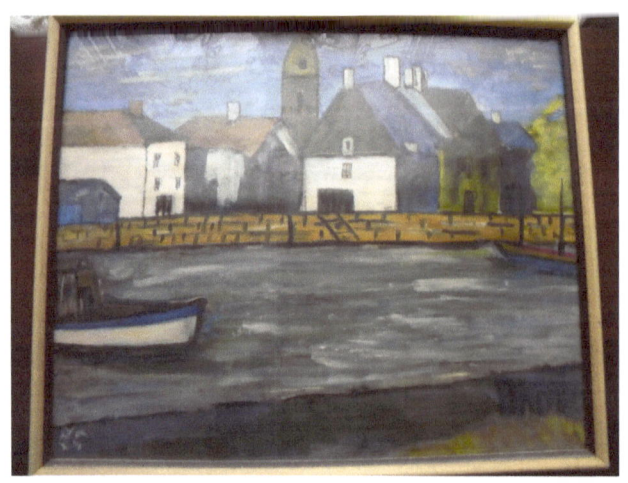

Jug of Bittersweet
N/A
Oil
23 1/4" x 29 1/4"
Collection of Elisabeth L. Austin and Chris Bibeau

Red Barn Theatre
N/A
Watercolor
17.5" x 11.5"
Collection of Suzi R. and John V. Austin

Dutch Canal
N/A
Oil
18" x 16"
Collection of Michael J. and Susan L. Ricks

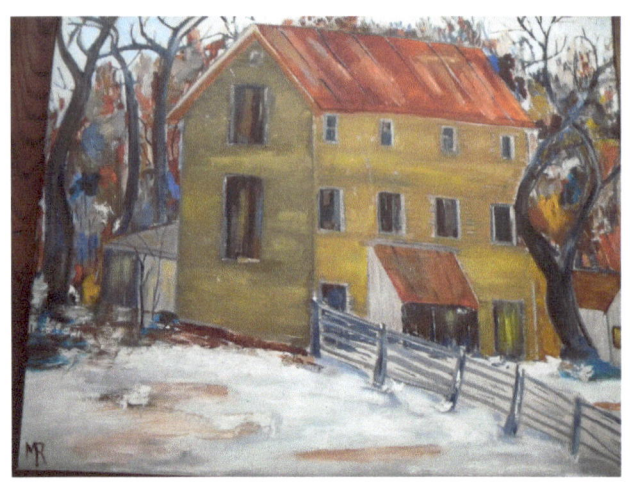

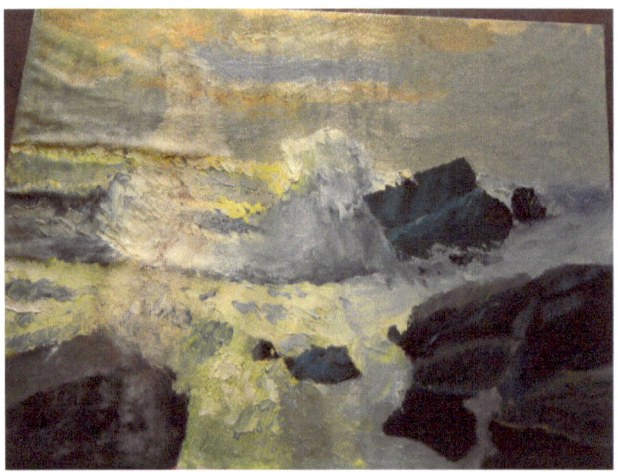

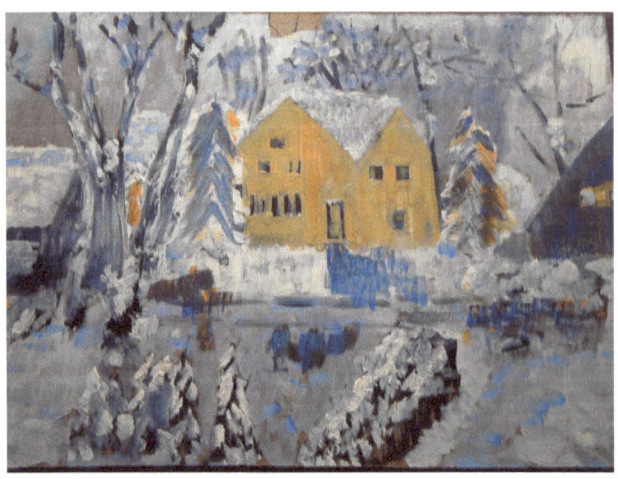

Brown Barn
N/A
Oil
30" x 24"
Collection of Michael J. and Susan L. Ricks

Ocean Rocks (Unfinished)
N/A
Watercolor (?)
18" x 16"
Collection of Michael J. and Susan L. Ricks

Wintertime Scene
N/A
Watercolor
18" x 16"
Collection of Michael J. and Susan L. Ricks

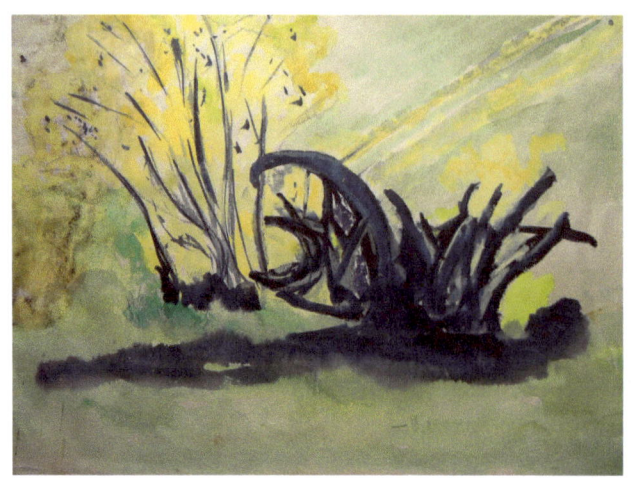

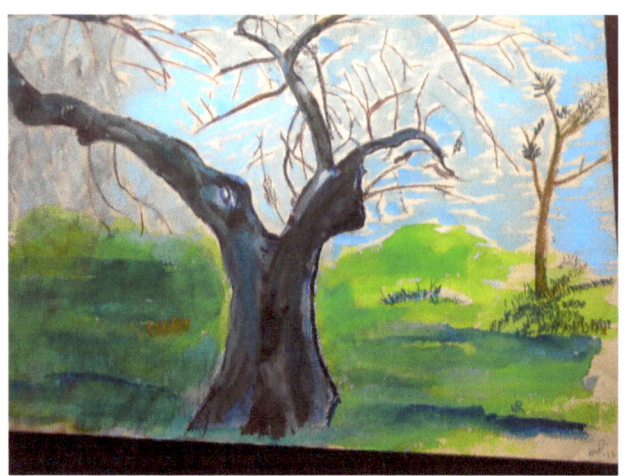

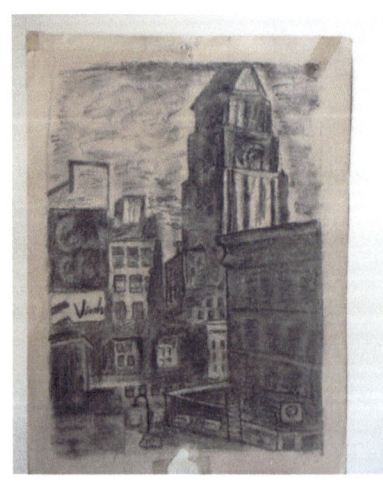

Pine Stump (Unfinished)
N/A
Watercolor
24" x 18"
Collection of Michael J. and Susan L. Ricks

Old Tree (Unfinished)
1962
Watercolor
24" x 18"
Collection of Michael J. and Susan L. Ricks

Street Light
1950's
Charcoal
8" x 12"
Collection of Thomas M. and Janice D. Ricks

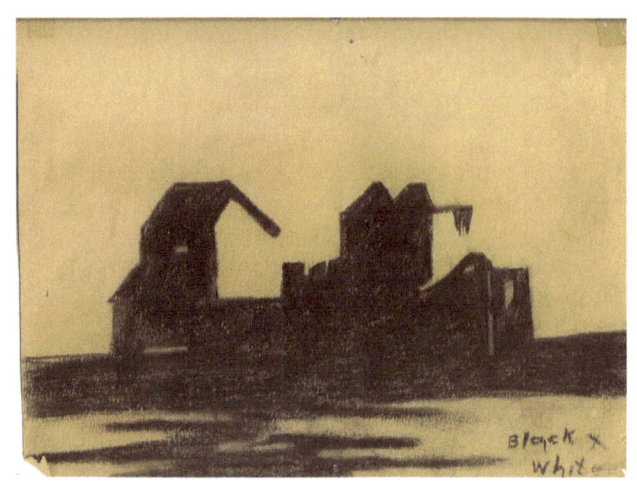

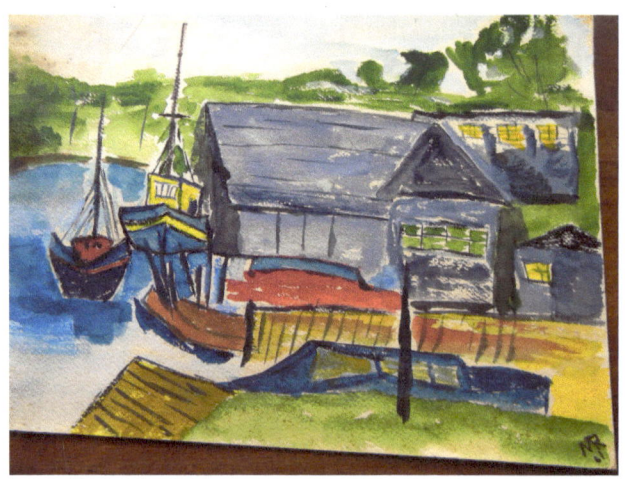

Grain Elavator
1952
Charcoal
11" x 8"
Collection of Thomas M. and Janice D. Ricks

Boat House
1961
Watercolor
18" x 12"
Collection of Michael J. and Susan L. Ricks

www.ingramcontent.com/pod-product-compliance
Lightning Source LLC
Chambersburg PA
CBHW040908180526
45159CB00010BA/2969